Brighton in the Fifties

Brigid Chapman

THE BOOK GUILD
25 HIGH STREET, LEWES

By the same author:

Weathervanes of Sussex
East Sussex Inns
West Sussex Inns
Royal Visitors to Sussex
Night of the Fires
The Surrey Quiz Book

First published in 1996 by The Book Guild, 25 High Street,
Lewes BN7 2LR

ISBN 1 85776 151 0

Designed and typeset by CGB, Lewes and printed in Great Britain by
Bookcraft (Bath) Ltd., Avon.

BRIGHTON IN THE FIFTIES

Contents

ACKNOWLEDGEMENTS

FOR much of the information and the photographs in this book I am indebted to the reporters and photographers of the *Brighton Herald*, the *Evening Argus*, the *Sussex Daily News* and the *Brighton Gazette* who covered the courts and the council meetings, the incidents, accidents and events of those days.

Brighton Reference Library kindly allowed me to use these photographs from its newspaper archives and its staff, especially Stephanie Green, gave me invaluable help.

I am also most grateful for the assistance I received with this project from John Roles, Senior Keeper (Curation) Brighton Museum, Melvyn Frankin, senior assistant in the Registry of Brighton Borough Council, Enrico Tedeschi of the Isetta Owners Club, and the staff of East Sussex Records Office in Lewes. Brighton Our Story Project kindly gave me permission to use a photograph of the Sussex Arts Ball from the Bubbles Ashdown Collection.

A big thank you, too, to Vernon Brand, for his invaluable total recall of the Fifties in Brighton and for photographs of the period from his personal collection. Also to Christopher and Judy Moore who probed their pre-marriage memories for me and provided what must be the most eye-brow raising wedding photograph of the decade.

INTRODUCTION

THE Fifties is a decade without a description. It was not swinging like the Sixties, strike torn like the Seventies, or enterprising like the yuppie Eighties. It started with rationing, curbs on spending, and with all kinds of materials in short supply as the Exchequer endeavoured to reduce the massive debt engendered by the war. It ended with the Chancellor taking ninepence off income tax, twopence off a pint of beer, reducing purchase tax and the Prime Minister, Harold Macmillan, claiming: 'Most of our people have never had it so good.'

In the years between there was the Cold War, the Korean War, Mau Mau terrorism, the Suez crisis. National Service was extended from eighteen months to two years, the Home Guard was revived, the Z Reservists were called up.

In 1951 there was the Festival of Britain with its Skylon and Dome of Discovery; in 1952 the utility mark was abolished and so were identity cards; in 1953 everyone watched the Coronation on their own or other people's black and white television sets. In 1954 Roger Bannister ran a mile in under four minutes and Billy Graham brought religion, American style, across the Atlantic to 180,000 people at Wembley Stadium.

In 1955 independent television was introduced and in 1956 came *Rock Around the Clock*, the film which created the youth culture that flower powered into the Sixties. It was also the year of Premium Bonds and £80,000 worth were sold over the counters in the Brighton postal district on the first day. In 1957 the Russians launched a husky called Laika into space in a Sputnik; in 1958 came the first MOT tests on cars ten year old and over; and in 1959 survey work started on the Channel Tunnel.

National events were reflected locally. Brighton marked the Festival of Britain with a splendid Regency exhibition at the Royal Pavilion and a pageant in the Great Arena at Preston Park depicting 2,000 years of history. It also built what was intended to be a popular addition to the sea front scene – the Western Bathing Pavilion. Just in time for the Coronation the Truleigh Hill relay transmitter opened and brought BBC TV to the town which was elaborately decorated in blues and golds and patriotically full of street parties.

During the decade Brighton lost its trolley buses, its locomotive works, several cinemas and theatres, a number of old established shops, much of its slum housing and its fish market from the arches on the lower esplanade.

It gained, by the 1951 Brighton Extension Act, large parts of the parishes of Stanmer and Falmer to bring the area of the borough up to a total of 14,347 acres. It also acquired a quantity of coffee bars and the Teddy Boys to go with them, its first supermarket, the Promettes, a number of tower blocks, a pre-fabricated public house, a factory assembling the BMW Isetta bubble car. For months it was the focus of national interest when the Chief Constable and two other police officers were arrested on bribery and conspiracy charges and committed for trial at the Old Bailey.

Here is one Sussex town's story of the forgotten Fifties, revealed through its newspapers and the photographs in them and through the recollections of some one-time residents. The year that started the decade began lightheartedly enough but ended in a distressing and frightening way – with an outbreak of smallpox.

1 A HAPPY NEW YEAR?

IN evening dress, and to the music of big bands, the people of Brighton danced their way into the 1950s. The second half of the twentieth century was welcomed with pre-war gusto by crowds round the Jubilee Clock Tower. Traffic had been diverted from the area and when the hands of the clock touched midnight the merrymakers linked arms to sing *Auld Lang Syne*, ships sounded their sirens, trains whistled, bells were rung. . .

Australian dancers Frank South and Muriel Watts set the mood for 500 revellers at the Metropole. At the Grand Hotel, when midnight struck, a little girl stepped from an oyster shell and tossed violets among the 600 or so dancers on the floor.

Business was brisk at Brighton's ballrooms. Queues formed at The Regent dance hall hours before it opened. When it did all tickets were sold within minutes and a capacity crowd of 1,200 danced in the decade to the music of Syd Dean and his augmented orchestra.

At the Aquarium ballroom Frank Weir and his band was on the rostrum as another 1,000 or so revellers waltzed and fox-trotted, danced the rhumba and samba, to such tunes of the time as *Red Roses for a Blue Lady, Put Your Shoes on Lucy, Begin the Beguine and Night and Day*. The Mayor and Mayoress, Alderman Ernest Marsh and his daughter, Dorothy Foulger, were among the guests of the Brighton branch of NALGO, which was marking the occasion with one of the last dances to be held at the Royal Pavilion.

A world war and its austerity aftermath had dominated the previous decade, and the austerity was by no means over on this New Year's Eve. A lot of food was still rationed, so were sweets, and soap. Licences had to be obtained before any

7

building work could be done, private car drivers were allowed petrol for just ninety miles motoring a month and there was a five shillings limit on meals served in hotels and restaurants. Paper was rationed and the size and circulation of newspapers limited to their pre-war levels.

Regardless of these restrictions Brightonians partied their way into the Fifties with hope in their hearts, smiles on their faces and glasses in their hands. . .

But a year that began so happily ended in fear. On December 29 came the shock announcement of one death from smallpox and three further cases confirmed. The following day three more patients were found to have the disease and queues formed outside the doctors' surgeries for vaccination.

There were another three confirmed cases on New Year's Eve and the Medical Officer of Health, Dr Rutherford Cramb, appealed to everyone who had visited Bevendean Hospital for Infectious Diseases between December 18 and 28 to come forward. Emergency vaccination centres were opened in the local area and 520 people were vaccinated on the first day at the one in Brighton.

On January 1 there was another case confirmed – a nurse at Bevendean. Next day there were four more – two nurses, one domestic and one laundry worker – and the hospital, which had been built during a nineteenth century outbreak of smallpox, was put in quarantine. Its sixty strong team of nursing and domestic staff was completely sealed off from any contact with the outside world except by telephone. Food was taken to a garage nearby from where it was later collected by hospital staff. Fortunately, considering the icy weather, the hospital had adequate supplies of coal.

Staff at the telephone exchange had to cope with a constant barrage of calls as people, not wishing to make contact in person, or choosing to write, tried to reach family and friends by

The 'no admittance' notices go up at Foredown Hospital, Portslade, opened to receive cases that could not be taken to Dartford because of the adverse weather conditions.

telephone. Post Office Telephones appealed to the public to restrict the number of calls made during peak hours because the hard pressed telephonists who were also suffering from the discomforts of vaccination.

On January 3 a second patient died and Foredown Isolation Hospital at Portslade was opened in case the wintry weather got worse and it became impossible to reach Dartford Isolation Hospital to which all previous confirmed cases had been transferred.

On January 5 two cases, one of them mild, were confirmed and two of the early cases discharged from Dartford. By January 13 the number of confirmed cases totalled twenty eight, of which seven, among them two children and a girl telephone operator at the Brighton exchange, had died of the disease. One of the features of smallpox is that a person can have a mild dose which can be transmitted to a contact in a most virulent form. This is apparently what happened at Brighton. Several patients who were mildly infected were at Bevendean Hospital for several days before a man whose symptoms were unmistakable, and who died a few hours after he had been taken ill, disclosed the true nature of their complaint.

A young RAF officer was the innocent cause of bringing the disease to Brighton from India. He was a lodger at the Kemp Street home of 53 year old Harold Bath, the first victim of the outbreak.

The Air Ministry's reaction was, in the circumstances, somewhat surprising. It cancelled, in the proof stage, the printing by a Brighton firm of 3,000 programmes for the Air Training Corps Boxing Championships at the Albert Hall. It also banned a Brighton cadet, who was a finalist, from taking part in the competition.

'The Air Ministry has done Brighton a great disservice,' claimed the *Sussex Daily News** leader writer. 'If the example of the RAF was followed the whole town would be brought to a standstill, which is absurd, impossible, and on the facts, totally unjustified.'

The Ministry of Health increased the feeling of alarm in the outside world by advising the National Union of Teachers to cancel its proposed conference at Brighton. A special delegates meeting, which should have brought more than 200 members of the National Union of Journalists to the Metropole was postponed 'as a precautionary measure, also on the advice of the Health Ministry'.

The Crusader Insurance Company's three day conference at the Grand Hotel was cancelled and British Manufactured Bearings of Crawley called off its annual children's party there. 'The children will be given presents instead,' said a spokesman for the firm.

Brighton was placed in virtual quarantine. Correspondents in national newspapers suggested letters should not be sent from the town's post office until the all clear was given, and Brightonians working away from home were shunned by their colleagues. A Sussex man sent to work at a refuse tip in Edmonton was dismissed within an hour as other employees had seen his card had been stamped at Brighton Labour Exchange and refused to work with him.

Football matches were cancelled and Brighton and Hove Wheelers Cycle Club had to call off its run to Waldron. 'We don't want you here,' they were told by their erstwhile hosts.

The discovery of a smallpox contact from Brighton at RAF Padgate in Lancashire resulted in the mass vaccination of all personnel at this basic training station. And everyone in the Crowborough area was vaccinated when it became known that a woman from Jarvis Brook, who had been to Brighton with a coach party from the village, was under observation at Foredown Hospital. She was found not to be suffering from the disease.

A lorry driver from the London factory of George Borwich and Sons claimed he had been told he could not deliver goods to Brighton as it was a closed area and if he got in he could not get out. Another instance of misinformation was revealed in a letter to the *Evening Argus*:

'It is with great displeasure that the nursing staff of Bevendean read that some of our members were climbing the hospital walls and coming into town,' it stated. 'We are all fully aware of the risks involved in nursing so virulent a disease as smallpox but we are here as volunteers and not as conscripted staff. Therefore it is highly unlikely that the quarantine ban and regulations have or will be deliberately broken.'

While outsiders panicked the people of Brighton took what

precautions they could, rolled up their sleeves to be vaccinated, and carried on. Two middle aged housewives, determined to do their bit, turned up with their nightwear and toothbrushes and volunteered to help in the laundry at Bevendean.

They were welcomed by the matron, Mabel Bennett, one of whose many problems during the hospital's thirty four day quarantine, was a shortage of domestic workers. 'Many of them were married women with domestic ties and they had, quite reasonably, remained outside the hospital gates when they closed three weeks ago,' she told the *Brighton Herald.*

'We ran the laundry with just four people, the head laundress, her assistant, and our two volunteer helpers working anything up to fourteen hours a day.

'Everyone helped out cheerfully with the cleaning and scrubbing during off duty hours. It was one of the recognised forms of recreation adopted by the nursing staff.'

When the all clear came on February 10, a total of 77,000 people had been vaccinated.

Matron Mabel Bennett

The outbreak had been limited to thirty five cases – ten of them fatal. Of those who died seven had never been vaccinated and the others not since infancy.

It could have been so much worse. After a woman patient had been taken to hospital health department staff found that her washing had been sent to a laundry in the locality which had 4,000 customers

They made this dread discovery at 10pm when the laundry was shut and the proprietor at his home, quite a distance from Brighton. Dr Cramb telephoned him, was given the name of his manageress and collected a key to the laundry from her. Then, with four health inspectors in protective clothing, he searched among the bundles of washing. At midnight the infected clothing was found, fortunately in a bundle which had not been unwrapped.

Brighton had coped with outbreaks of smallpox before. There was a serious epidemic, also in the winter months, 175 previously. It was not confined to a particular area but broke out 'in Several Different Places in the Town at once' which put a heavy burden on the parish purse as it cost £6 to move each person to the pest house.

The inhabitants decided at a public meeting on January 25 1785 that 'it appearing Impossible to Prevent the Infection from Becoming General It was Agreed for the Poor in the Town House and such other of the Inhabitants of said Town to be inoculated as should be Deemed Proper.'

A committee was appointed to conduct the inoculation of the poor at the expense of the parish. It went about it in a businesslike way, first finding out 'the Numbers of Persons who Had the Small Pox and those who Had Not had the same in said Town.'

A survey showed that 1,733 people had previously had the disease and 1,887 had not. 'In consequence of the foregoing the inoculation commenced on the 27 of Jany and in Course of a few Day's the aforesaid number of Eighteen Hundred and Eighty Seven were Inoculated – Persons of all ages from One Day to Near Fourscore Years Old,' says the Vestry Book.

There were plans to move the 'birdcage' bandstand by the West Pier and the trippers' favourite ice cream and chips outlets from the arches on the lower esplanade.

Improvements to the race course were appreciated by its patrons. More than 123,000 paid for admission to the enclosure in the 1952 season – 8,000 up on the previous year.

2 THE BEST LAID SCHEMES

WHEN the smallpox scare was over Brighton went back to the business of catering for holidaymakers – preferably ones with money to spend. Before the war people of leisure had been attracted by its culture and character, its top class class hotels, its West End style restaurants and entertainments and its three golf courses. It also had the reputation of being the place to go for discreet weekends of dalliance and/or divorce and it was never short of day trippers.

Londoners by the thousand came by the train and coachload on bank holidays and summer weekends to pack the piers, the amusements arcades, fill the deck chairs on the promenades, snooze on the beach and, if it were warm enough, swim in the sea.

But had the war changed people's holiday habits? 'How will we bring them back to our stony beaches when they have seen Paree, Capri, Sidi Barani?' wondered hoteliers and restaurant owners and others whose livelihood depended on the tourist trade. And who should they woo, who try to attract? Some wanted to concentrate almost entirely on day trippers; others thought the future lay with foreign visitors; there was a strong lobby for conferences and trade fairs.

Everyone had ideas for the town's future development. The council even set up an Ideas Committee and its Planning Committee, Entertainments Committee, Markets Committee, individual members, chief officers and local business and trade organisations all came up with suggestions.

One man whose plans were constantly making headlines was Lewis Cohen (later Lord Cohen) a Labour member since 1930 of a council which was to remain staunchly Conservative until 1986. He was Brighton born and educated and, in 1929,

The mayor making of 1955 with Cllr Lewis Cohen receiving his chain of office from the retiring mayor, Jasper Leek.

at the age of thirty two, became secretary of the Brighton and Sussex Building Society. Four years later he was its managing director and, after the post war name change to the Alliance Building Society he became its chairman and managing director. Lewis Cohen was politically, as well as administratively active in the Fifties, contesting the Kemp Town parliamentary seat for Labour three times.

One of his earliest, and least practical schemes, was to extend Valley Gardens from St Peter's Church to Preston Park 'so that from Knoyle Road to the sea a chain of gardens would run right through the valley of the town'.

The planners vetoed this one immediately on the grounds of cost which, considering the number of properties which would have to be acquired and demolished, would be enormous.

Lewis Cohen's other ideas were more viable. Describing his vision to Brighton Rotarians in 1951 he insisted that to ensure prosperity the town must attract visitors all the year round and it must be planned as both a residential and holiday resort. He listed among projects for the future:

> A conference hall, concert hall, flats and shopping arcades on land between West Street and Russell Square, an area cleared for development before the war.
> A new open air bathing pool in the town centre.
> More modern hotels.
> A bathing plage to the west of the West Pier.
> A children's playground and music pavilion on the sea front.
> Sun terraces on Madeira Drive in place of the existing coach parks.
> A small harbour for yachtsmen and better facilities for youth hostellers.

Brighton's borough surveyor, D J Howe, had other ideas. His long term plan took into account the town's present and anticipated parking problems as well as providing attractions for both residents and visitors. He wanted:

> Dual carriageways 30ft wide separated by 6ft wide islands planted with decorative shrubs, stretching the length of the sea front from the Aquarium to the Hove boundary.
>
> Underground parking for 950 cars in parks beneath the gardens in Regency Square, under King's Road at West Street, beneath the new town hall and near the fish market.
>
> Two main shopping arcades, one at the lower end of Queensbury Mews on a side of the Metropole Hotel and the other between the lower end of East Street and Pool Valley.
>
> An underground bathing station, a restaurant and shops between the bandstand and the Palace Pier.
>
> A standard size bathing pool and a children's pool at or near the entrance to the West Pier.

Alderman A V Nicholls suggested that Madeira Drive, from the eastern end of the Aquarium to Paston Place, should be covered over by extending the existing terrace and putting on it ornamental gardens, a bandstand, solarium, and a children's playground. The area underneath could be used as a car park. He estimated these additional attractions would bring in £50,000 a year – the product of a sixpenny rate.

An even more ambitious plan for a five acre pleasure park on the lines of Margate's Dreamland beneath the cliffs at Black Rock was rejected by the council. The cost, it was told, 'without refinement or equipment' would be £50,000 an acre.

During his mayoralty in 1952 Alderman Eric Simms came up with an instant solution to the town's lack of conference accommodation. 'Buy the Festival of Britain's Dome of Discovery and use it as a conference hall,' he said.

When it considered the estimated cost – anything from

£250,000 to £750,000 to remove the structure from the South Bank site; to transport, re-erect and adapt it; the council shook its head.

It shook its collective head to a number of other schemes too, but surprisingly got quite excited about a plan to turn the Royal Pavilion into a casino. It went so far as to ask the Government to amend the licensing laws and the betting and gaming acts in the interests of the holiday trade.

Four years later the Home Secretary informed the council that the Royal Commission on betting, gaming and lotteries favoured some amendments but not to permit gaming casinos in this country. Members of the Regency Society heaved a sigh of relief. They had opposed the plan from the start.

The conference hall issue took on a new urgency when the Labour Party decided not to hold its 1959 conference at the Sports Stadium as planned. Delegates to the 1957 conference had complained of cold feet. Not surprising, really, as they were sitting above an ice rink.

The Conservatives, it seemed, were made of sterner stuff. They confirmed their booking for October of that year.

Calls for a first class hall for conferences suddenly came flooding in from all quarters – the chamber of commerce, the Brighton Auctioneers Association, the hoteliers, faced with a £100,000 loss of trade because of Labour's cancellation. Lewis Cohen appealed to the council to sink all its political differences and think positively about the town's future.

It had thought positively in January 1952 although there was no conference hall included in the scheme it passed for double tier terracing on the lower promenade, a bandstand and model boating pool opposite the sea end of West Street, a winter garden with an underground car park at the bottom of West Street, an open air swimming pool near the West Pier and terraced promenades on Madeira Drive and Marine Parade with coach parks and coach station facilities.

This, like so many other plans, came to nothing as a result of Government restrictions on local authority spending.

In April that year work started on what was to be the only development by the council on the sea front during the decade. At a cost of £13,000 a bathing pavilion with changing facilities for 2,000 was built between the putting green and boating pool beyond the West Pier.

It was formally opened in 1952 as one of Brighton's contributions to the Festival of Britain but was not a success. Local swimmers shunned it, preferring to change free of charge on the beach, and the foreign visitors it was intended to please chose to swim in warmer seas. In 1957 it was leased to the Milk Marketing Board and turned into a milk bar and cafe.

The Western Bathing Pavilion as it is today, boarded up and abandoned.

3 ON THE HOMES FRONT

MUCH as it wanted to upgrade its sea front shop window the council had even more pressing and immediate demands upon it. Like almost every other town in the country Brighton had a housing problem. Between July 1940 and March 1944 there had been fifty six air raids in which more than 200 houses had been totally destroyed, 894 seriously damaged and 10,498 slightly damaged.

German bombers always tended to target areas of maximum population density. In consequence they accelerated the slum clearance programme begun in the 1930s in Albion Hill, Carlton Hill and around Edward Street. But this was small consolation to the dispossessed and the men and women back from the war to family and friends and, with a bit of luck, to their old job. They needed somewhere to live, and to begin with only the council had the power to provide homes by issuing the necessary building licences.

New estates of houses, flats and some pre-fabs were built as speedily as possible at Hollingbury, Moulescoomb, Coldean, Whitehawk, Woodingdean and Patcham. In all 500 pre-fabs, which came in sections on the backs of lorries, were put up in various parts of the town. There was even a pre-fabricated pub, the County Oak on the corner of Carden Hill and County Oak Avenue.

What the *Brighton Gazette* described as 'Hollingbury housing estate's very own local,' was opened by the then mayor, Alderman Samuel Davey, in September 1950. It was a Whitbreads house and its licensee was Charles Frederick Worthington. 'And, yes, the brewery has forgiven me for my surname,' he said.

The pub was simply two adjacent V-roofed pre-fabs, one used as a saloon bar, the other as a public bar. Each had a

Hollingbury branch library now occupies the pre-fab which was, until Whitbreads built a new house on the adjoining site, the County Oak pub.

wide front porch and the two were linked by cross beams.

The whole structure was painted white and there were flower gardens at the sides and rear. Towering above the building was an inn sign mounted on a tall wooden pillar. It had been designed by Violet Rutter, great granddaughter of the man who founded and managed Brighton's first gas supply, and depicted the oak tree at Crawley which marks the county boundary between Sussex and Surrey.

The inn sign is still there today, outside the licensed premises of more orthodox appearance which replaced the temporary County Oak in the early Sixties. So is the pre-fab, now long past it ten year shelf life but doing duty as Hollingbury's branch library. It looks a little different, but not much, from when it was first put up. The two porches have gone and been replaced by a central entrance and recently it has had a new roof.

Not all were as happy with their new homes as the people of Hollingbury were with their pre-fab pub. Although the rents were modest – tenants of one bedroom flats on the new Bates estate in Lewes Road paid an inclusive rent of twenty one shillings (£1.05p) per week; the two bedroom flats were let at 24s 6d (£2.22½p) a week and the elderly could rent apartments for 17s 6d (87½p) a week – they were on the outskirts of the town.

Workers who before the war had lived conveniently close to their jobs complained of the financial burden of the bus fares from the outlying estates. Their situation got worse as fuel prices continued to rise.

There was a desperate shortage of building land even though some allotment holders had been dispossessed, and playing fields and other open spaces compulsorily purchased. By 1952, with still more than 5,000 people on the waiting list for homes, the council was talking about the need for satellite towns and Peacehaven, Hassocks and Keymer were named as possibles. Brighton's net debt was £19,232,366 or £65 8s 2d per head of the population of 155,600. Nearly half this sum was borrowings to build houses.

The relaxation of building controls in 1954 increased the development of new estates of bungalows and houses by the private sector. These properties sold almost before the plans were off the drawing board and by the end of 1958 the supply of building land was practically exhausted.

In Brighton, as elsewhere, the planners took the high rise option to compensate for the shortage of space. The first six storey block of twenty six flats – 'each with many desirable features and easy to run' – was opened on the Bristol estate at East Kemp Town in January 1958.

The civic party, headed by the mayor, Alderman Charles

Tyson, took the lift up to the top floor to meet Hilda Woodford who, with her husband, had moved in from Somerset Road. 'She was full of praise for all that the accommodation has to offer including the sea view across to the two piers to Worthing and beyond,' said the *Brighton Herald.*

The following year a start was made on the Albion Hill redevelopment scheme in which there were blocks of flats up to eleven storeys high replacing the old tenements. The planners' intention was 'to provide 426 dwellings in a self contained community in the heart of modern Brighton, with its own shops and social amenities and with provision for religious activities.

'Around the eight and eleven storey blocks will be large areas of open space planted with trees and grass, and in their semi-basements there will be clubs and community centres.'

This high living dream began to come true in 1961 when the town's first eleven storey tower block – called, rather obviously, Highleigh – was opened by the mayor, Alan Johnson. Another half dozen sprang up around it on Albion Hill in the next four years.

Landlords with old properties let at uneconomic rents welcomed the Rent Act which came into force in 1957 but tenants on low incomes were badly hit by it. Elderly couples who had lived in the same house or flat since their wedding day, probably paying rent throughout that period to the same landlord, found themselves faced with a swingeing increase if the landlord chose to improve the property. For many it was a case of pay up or get out.

Brighton had a fair share of old and dilapidated privately rented housing. It also had someone only too willing to champion the cause of those likely to be dispossessed.

Harry Cowley, known as 'the bowler hatted champion of the underdog' was a chimney sweep from the Albion Hill area who liked nothing better than battling against bureaucracy.

The tower blocks on Albion Hill, on which work began in 1959, as they look today.

Among the many causes he espoused was that of homeless ex-servicemen and women. After the First World War he formed the Brighton Vigilantes, a group which succeeded in fixing up ex-soldiers and their families in empty properties and negotiating with the landlords for them to pay a fair rent.

He was about to revive the group in 1945 to deal with another post war housing shortage but at about the same time a law was passed which enabled local authorities to requisition houses that had been empty for eighteen or more months and install homeless families in them.

Pensioners came out in force when Harry organised a meeting.

When the Rent Act came along Harry Cowley and the Vigilantes took to the streets again. He took a group from Brighton to a protest meeting in Trafalgar Square and wrote to the Queen asking her to intervene as 'much hardship is likely to accrue from this unpopular Act of Legislation . . . which would undoubtedly produce many homeless British Citizens, among whom regrettably would be included many old and feeble people'.

He organised a series of local protest meetings, one of them outside the home of an eighty nine year old blind man given notice to quit a house for which he had been paying an inclusive rent of 8s 6d (32½p) a week. The new rent, which he could not afford to pay, was £1 14s (£1.70p) exclusive of rates.

Harry, by that time a pensioner himself, also campaigned vigorously on behalf of senior citizens, pressing for an increase in the old age pension from £2 to £3 a week and for half price train and bus fares for them.

Just how close to the poverty line some pensioners were was revealed in the *Brighton Herald's* report of an Upper Gardner Street Traders Association's New Year Party for old people at the Corn Exchange in 1955. One of the guests, eighty three year old widow Mary Bungay, had pawned her wedding ring to pay for her Christmas dinner.

'Out of £3 a week pension and national assistance there is not much left for food when half of it has to go on rent and there is electric light, coal and gas to pay for from the remaining thirty shillings,' she said. 'I wanted something nice to eat for Christmas so decided to pawn my wedding ring. I got ten shillings for it and planned to save sixpence or a shilling a week to get it back.'

But Mary, who worked as a cook in Worthing until she was eighty two, did not have to save up and wait for weeks to get her ring back. *Herald* readers, touched by her story, came to her aid. One sent the paper a ten shilling note for her to redeem the ring – which she did straightaway.

A fine summer bank holiday with more people than pebbles on
the beach and, below, all the year round swimmers take
their traditional Christmas Day dip.

4 ON HOLIDAY

THE first Whitsun bank holiday of the Fifties was, like the New Year's Eve celebrations, of pre-war proportions. The weather was good and the unexpected removal of petrol rationing brought thousands out in their cars.

Six weeks previously the price of petrol had been raised in the budget by ninepence to three shillings a gallon. At the same time the ration for private motorists had been doubled to 180 miles a month. After that announcement nobody expected to hear a few weeks later that petrol rationing would end entirely in time for Whitsun.

From Friday evening the influx began and by Saturday there were problems with parking. Motoring organisations reported more than 4,000 cars an hour making the homeward journey on the A23 on Whit Monday evening. 'But money was tight,' said the traders.

Another restriction lifted in time for the holiday weekend was the five shilling limit on meals in all hotels, restaurants and catering establishments. It had come into force in June 1942 and, as well as price, limited the number of courses and stipulated what may be served as a main dish.

But this did not mean a free for all on the food front. There was rationing until 1954 when, on July 14, meat was the last item to be freed. The address of the Food Office - it was at 166 Western Road - was included in the official guides until then, just in case a visitor had mislaid his or her ration book. . .

By the summer of 1953 holidaymakers were in more of a spending mood. The crowds which doubled the population of Brighton to give it the best August Bank Holiday since the war were described by a publicity department spokesmen as 'a good natured, well behaved, free spending lot'. Many of them had to sleep on the beach because there was not a bed to be had.

There was a fear that the rail strike due to start on the Sunday evening would affect the Whitsun of 1955. Caterers such as Marwins with a 250 seater restaurant in the King's Road Arches, did lose business. It offered discounts to pensioners and ex-service associations and specialised in large works', business and children's outings, many of which were cancelled because of the strike.

The council's takings were sixty six per cent down on previous post war years and sea front shops and cafes reported a seventy five per cent drop in trade. Only £39 was realised from the hire of deck chairs.

Blazing sunshine, soaring temperatures and the start of new premier Harold Macmillan's 'never had it so good' era made the 1957 August Bank Holiday far the best of the decade.

An incredible 95,000 people went through the turnstiles of the Palace Pier, 50,000 on to the West Pier. There was not a spare inch of space on the beaches when the tide was in and the council's total takings were £6,000 plus with the receipts at the Black Rock pool up by 100 per cent. There were no complaints – happy days were here again.

If the weather forecasts for a summer bank holiday were good the council would leave 2,000 deckchairs out at night for 'latecomers with accommodation difficulties'. It would also open up the beach and promenade annexe beneath the Palace Pier to give any *al fresco* sleepers a bit of shelter should the Meteorological Office forecast be wrong and the weather change.

In the interests of safety an additional clause was introduced to the Litter and Refuse byelaws to stop vandals leaving broken glass on the beach after shying stones at empty bottles as if they were coconuts. Maximum penalty, if caught,

Pretty girls on parade. Five of Brighton's first six Promettes pose for photographs on the lower esplanade.

was a fine of £5.

Another council sponsored addition to the sea front scene took the svelte form of six 'glamour girls' wearing distinctive badges and carrying specially designed handbags containing little books with details of the town's amenities and bus and train timetables. They were on the promenade at weekends to answer visitors' questions, 'doing the job for expenses only'. said the publicity department, which had named them Promettes.

By 1956 the girls were in mist blue uniforms with cerise piping and carrying lighters as well as the town guidebook in smart new shoulder bags complete with a pocket for their make up.

The lighters, explained the *Brighton Herald,* were for lighting other people's cigarettes. A strict no smoking rule applied to Promettes on duty.

The six, readers were told, favoured short hair styles with their perky forage caps. They trained for their weekend duties at the Vogue Mannequin School and wore white gloves to match the detachable white collars on their suit reveres, and black suede shoes.

They had white pullovers to wear under their summer weight fabric uniforms on cold days and the outfit was completed by a raincoat of black nylon, striped in cerise and green. The Promettes' caravan headquarters was parked on the sea front between the piers and there foreign visitors could have their questions answered in French, German, Italian and Spanish.

The following year the girls had new uniforms – pencil slim skirts and middy jackets in clerical grey piped with crimson, air hostess type hats and crimson bags and white gloves. All were more than 5ft 7ins tall and chosen, said the publicity department, 'for their appearance, charm, tact and knowledge of one or more foreign languages'.

The Promettes became a much photographed feature of the sea front and in 1959 three of them, Jill Davenport, Maureen Galloway and Elizabeth Southgate, were pictured taking turkeys for a walk along the promenade to publicise the British Turkey Federation's campaign to increase the consumption of turkey at Easter.

Not so popular were the Beachniks. These disciples of American beat writers Allen Ginsberg and Jack Kerouac, known elsewhere as Beatniks, expressed their dissatisfaction with modern materialism by ignoring it. They had a liking for LSD and sharing everything – food, money, sex – but they paid little attention to personal hygiene.

They would sit on the beach all day bundled up in army surplus greatcoats and torn jeans, regardless of the heat of the summer sun. Occasionally a group of them would amble down to the water's edge and, fully clothed, take a dip in the sea. They considered they were making a serious social protest but the rest of the people taking their ease on Brighton's beaches, which they were infesting in the late Fifties, thought they were a nasty nuisance.

However, they were not breaking any beach bylaw by simply sitting on the shingle and scratching themselves – so how could they be removed? The council did the only thing possible, it washed them away. Nightly gangs of workmen would hose down the shingle above the high tide mark – in the interest of general cleanliness, it was said.

An earlier infestation had not proved so easy to remove. In 1953 beaches all along the coast were plagued by swarms of

Housing Minister Harold Macmillan with Alderman Samuel Hay, right, and Howard Johnson, MP for Kemp Town, far left, and council officials watching the spraying operation.

black and brown flies. Representatives of the affected resorts held an emergency conference at Worthing to see what could be done about them and Brighton sent some specimens to the natural history department of the British Museum. There the flies were identified as two varieties of *coelopa* which feed on rotting seaweed.

The council's cleansing department experimented with a variety of insecticides to spray them away. When it found the most effective one the chemical was delivered by Land Rover. The vehicle, towing an industrial spraying machine, was driven across flexible boarding laid on the shingle.

By this ingenious method a large area could be covered in a single operation and Harold Macmillan, then Minister of Housing and Local Government, came to see for himself how the job was done. The work went on throughout the winter and it was not until the Easter of 1954 that the beaches were completely free of the flies.

They were back again three years later, accompanied by some waterborne nasties – Portugese men of war. These jelly-fish inflicted painful stings on anyone unfortunate enough to tread on them and squads of council workmen were sent out morning and evening to destroy all they could find on the beach.

**Open air art shows gave a Left Bank look to the sea front.
Exhibitors had to pay 1s 6d and draw lots for display space.**

5 ON THE SEA FRONT

BRIGHTON did well by its holidaymakers and day trippers during the decade. Waiting for them on the sea front, where they headed straight from trains, coaches and their cars, were all kinds of seaside entertainments. The two piers were both flourishing, their wartime severances from the shore now only a memory.

The West Pier, built to the design of Eugenius Birch and opened in 1866, stretched 1,115ft out to sea. It still retained an air of Victorian propriety, although its repertory theatre had been converted into an amusement arcade and anglers occupied the landing stages used before the war by steamships making day trips to France.

It was rather more of a residents' than a visitors' pier. Brightonians liked to take their ease on the free side seating or on the benches under the canopies of the central windbreak, have lunch or tea in the 600 seater Ocean Restaurant or listen to Harry Groombridge and his orchestra in the concert hall where often fashion shows or beauty contests were staged.

In the summer of 1950 regular pier promenaders became accustomed to seeing a young man casually dive off the side seating at the pier's highest point, swim to the Palace Pier and then swim back to the ladder at the West Pier's landing stage. Twice a week, always at the same time of day regardless of the weather or the state of the tide, the young man did his dive.

What the watchers did not know was that the mother of this fourteen year old schoolboy, John Morris, was running along the beach between the

Between the piers swimmer John Morris.

piers clutching his clothes while he was in the water.

His younger sisters, Judy and Janet, sat by the paddling pool rolling about with laughter at this manifestation of maternal concern. 'She thought he might get tired and come ashore and she did not want him to catch cold,' recalled Judy, forty five years on. 'John is still a fitness fanatic but now it is running not swimming. He completed last year's London Marathon in a good time.'

Another magnet for day trippers was the lower esplanade

with its gift shops, cafes, ice cream parlours, whelk stalls and rock shops. There were rowboats for hire on the beach, deckchairs everywhere and a wholesale fish market which operated from 216 to 224 King's Road Arches.

When not occupied by stalls selling dabs, cod, whiting, plaice, and other species of fish in season the hard in front of the fish market was a favourite place for political meetings and anyone who wished to stand on a soapbox and address an audience.

It became a battleground for conflicting political ideologies whenever municipal or parliamentary elections were pending. Some of these wars of words became so acrimonious that periodically one or other of the opposing parties vowed not to take part in them. They never stayed away for long.

In 1960 the fish market was moved to a new extension of the municipal market in Circus Street, much to the annoyance of the fishermen and the residents and visitors. They liked to watch the catches being sold by Dutch auction with its cries of 'Has 'em' and to be part of a scene dating back to Domesday. New hygiene regulations caused the move, combined with councillors' concern that the smell of fish, and even the sight of them, might offend some holidaymakers.

The Palace Pier, all 1,650 foot of it, had an amusements hall with every sort of slot machine, including the ones that irritatingly let go of an object once it had been skillfully caught in the jaws of its crane, so depriving the player of, perhaps, a bottle of scent, a box with a ten shilling note taped to it, or a brooch or similar gewgaw pinned to a card.

There were elaborate shooting galleries, a helter skelter, ghost train, dodgems and booths in which fortunes were told, palms read, and crystal balls consulted to see what the future had in store.

The paddle steamer *Glen Gower* could be boarded from the pier's landing stage for trips along the coast and, from 1954,

37

Passengers board the PS *Glen Gower* for the first postwar no passport trip to Boulogne

for no passport trips to Boulogne. The first of these trips included a group of civic dignitaries, intent on forming an *entente cordiale* with their opposite numbers in France, and a party of Teddy Boys intent of having a good time.

The two groups clashed almost as soon as they stepped ashore. The Teds, behaving rowdily, turned up at the cafe where the councillors were being entertained by their French hosts. The official party left the premises hastily, to avoid any possible embarassment.

Two of the young no passport trippers nearly got left behind – and three did. As the paddler steamer cast off for the return trip two Teddy Boys rushed down the jetty waving their arms wildly and shouting 'wait for us! wait for us!'. The steamer back paddled to pick them up. The three who totally missed the boat spent the night in Boulogne and were sent home the next day.

On summer evenings and on matinee days audiences made the long walk from the shore to the 1,400 seater theatre at the pier head to see either a summer show - Clarkson Rose's Twinkle and the Fol-de-Rols with Jack Tripp were great favourites - a touring company production, or an offering from the resident repertory company.

The 500 yard totter over the slatted wooden decking was difficult for women wearing high heeled shoes. Regular patrons carried a change of footwear with them and the pier management thoughtfully provided wheel chairs, and uniformed attendants to push them, for any elderly stars of the theatrical firmament who might be heading the cast of current comedy or drama.

Another popular centre of entertainment was the nearby Aquarium, another Eugenius Birch building considerably modernised in the late 1920s by borough engineer David Edwards. It had been requisitioned by the RAF during the war but was now back in business with dancing, bars, a restaurant, a children's playground and amusements on the sun terraces. In the aquarium itself there were more than 2,000 marine specimens and there were guest appearances from chimpanzees Steve and Gordon.

Or what about a mile long trip on the Volk's Railway across the beach and sea to the open air swimming pool at Black Rock? This first public electric railway in the country, opened in 1883, was up and running after its wartime close down. The track had been renewed and a new station built for it at Peter Pan's Playground.

Often there was a chance to see someone attempting to beat all previous records for some feat of endurance or danger. Fasting was one of the favourites.

In 1952 holidaymakers could, on payment of one shilling, see the Irish American hypnotist, Jack Wafer, sealed up in a glass walled case measuring 11ft by 7ft at 40 Queens Road.

Youngsters at the council run Peter Pan's Playground, now a privately operated children's leisure park.

The feat he was attempting was to go without food for more than fifty nine days. Instead of eating, he was going to drink 120 syphons of soda water and smoke 3,600 cigarettes. The object of this unhealthy exercise was to win bets of £6,000 and £2,000 and beat the existing record for fasting.

The *Brighton Herald* reported briefly on October 31 that Jack had come of his glass case having been without food for seventy six days, lost a total of 1st 7lbs (9.52kg) in weight and won his bets.

Four years later White Yogi Michael Blondini could be seen for a shilling 'buried in a glass coffin' on the Palace Pier. He too was trying to establish a new world fasting record but his success or failure is not recorded.

6 SHIP TO SHORE

A TWELVE year old boy swam ashore from a grounded yacht with his pet kitten lashed to a cushion on a stormy August night in 1951. This was the first act in a beached boat drama which posed problems for the council and drew crowds of onlookers to the fish market hard almost daily for nearly two years.

The 25 ton ketch, *Rustler,* had anchored between the piers off Brighton after putting the owner's wife, Doreen Maitland, ashore at Shoreham where she was going to spend the night because of gale warnings. Aboard were Kenneth Maitland from Upnor, near Rochester; his son, Roger; a friend, Dennis Austin, also from Upnor; two dogs and the kitten.

When the wind got up to gale force, which it did some hours later, Kenneth Maitland tried to sail the ketch out to sea and to safety, but without success. He dropped anchor again but the anchor chain broke, and a huge wave caught the boat and flung it up on to the beach.

'After we ran aground the animals got frightened,' hero of the hour Roger told the *Sussex Daily News.* 'They were running around the deck in panic. We threw the dogs, Susan and Rastus, overboard as we knew they could swim ashore. We didn't know what to do with the kitten. Dad suggested tying her to the cushion and I swam ashore pushing it in front me.'

For this act of bravery it was suggested that Roger should be recommended for the White Cross, an award given to people who risk their lives to rescue an animal.

A week later, on the highest spring tide, an attempt was made to refloat *Rustler.* High water was at midnight and crowds gathered to watch but the ketch resisted all efforts to tow her free and remained stuck fast on the beach in front of the fish market.

And there she stayed until May 1953.

In September 1951 the borough council served a notice on Kenneth Maitland, who had camped out beside the boat to protect her from pilferers, requiring him to remove her from its beach.

On December 12 it wrote again asking how and when he planned to move the vessel. He replied to the effect that he was doing all he could but had to wait for suitable weather and tide conditions 'to enable Mr Tidy to use a bulldozer and to pull the boat down the beach and refloat her'.

The council's next move was to offer the Maitlands Arch No 250 to store whatever gear they wished to take off the vessel. At least with most of her fittings removed the owner would not have to camp beside her all winter under unsightly sheets of canvas.

It then called for reports from three marine engineers on the cost and feasibility of refloating *Rustler*. When these reports came in each said it was going to cost around £1,000 to make the ketch seaworthy and refloat her. She would need to be winched upright, fitted into a cradle, the hull re-caulked and then pulled over the shingle on an improvised slipway of greased timbers into the water.

Where was the money going to come from? The vessel, which had a four cylinder Brooks auxiliary engine, was valued at £19,000 but was not covered by insurance. The Maitlands could not afford to foot the bill. The council was not keen to do so.

By August 1952, although still a tourist attraction, the boat was becoming increasingly derelict and councillors were expressing their concern about it being a danger to people using the beach. Legally, while her owner was making attempts to refloat her, she could not be treated as flotsam and/or jetsam and disposed of accordingly.

There was some local sympathy for the Maitlands. Mrs Robinson of St Peter's Rectory, Hove informed the council in September that an appeal was being launched for funds to save the boat. But another winter came and went, during which time attempts to sell the hulk as scrap came to nothing, as did the fund raising efforts. At the end of April, after heavy seas had penetrated her hull, Kenneth Maitland finally abandoned his boat.

At 5.30am on Thursday May 7, 1953, watched by a large crowd, council workmen poured 120 gallons of paraffin onto *Rustler*. Three matches were struck and she was engulfed in a sheet of flame and soon reduced to ashes. Her metal keel, which had broken off, was carted away. The whole clearance operation cost £69. 6s. 4d.

7 THE REGENCY REVIVAL

THE boarding houses, the cafes and the amusement arcades had plenty of patrons but the big hotels were bothered. The well-to-do families who used to spend two or three weeks complete with children and their nannies beside the English seaside were now holidaying abroad, attracted by guaranteed sunshine, an advantageous exchange rate and unrationed food.

Conference delegates were arriving, but out of season and in no great numbers. The trade fairs and exhibitions which were later to supply plenty of expense account guests had not yet set up their stands at the Dome and the Corn Exchange.

Hoteliers were particularly depressed after the Festival of

Britain summer of 1951. The year had started with a smallpox epidemic. No sooner was that over than income tax was raised by sixpence, bringing the standard rate up to 9s.6d (47½p) in the £. At the same time Chancellor Hugh Gaitskell imposed a fifty per cent charge on previously free false teeth and spectacles and doubled the purchase tax on cars to sixty six and a half per cent.

'We are operating on the barest margin of profit and still holidaymakers are finding the charges beyond their means,' Brighton Hotels and Restaurant Association members were told by their chairman. 'There is a general shortage of money. We can only hope that new restrictions on tourist allowances for foreign travel will induce visitors to come to British resorts rather than go abroad.'

The Blenheim, one of the town's oldest hotels, closed its doors at the end of the year. It was sold to become offices. Harrisons Hotel was converted into flats, the Belvedere Mansions offered as business premises and the Adelphi Hotel, where Liberal Prime Minister William Ewart Gladstone often spent a holiday in the 1880s, when it was know at The Lion Mansion, was also redeveloped. One prospective purchaser wanted to turn it into offices but the planning committee felt it would be 'more appropriate' to convert it into first class flats.

The Exeter and the Hollywood on the sea front were, like the Royal York, used by borough council staff as annexes to the Town Hall. The Ministry of National Insurance Offices occupied the Chichester Mansions Hotel.

Even the 328 bedroom Metropole, which was the biggest hotel in the country outside London when it was built in 1890, was negotiating in 1952 to sell off one wing. The building was at the time considered 'too large for the patronage which is available to it'.

The council was concerned about the state of the hotel

trade for it was a major contributor to the rate revenue and one of the biggest employers of labour in the locality. There was the fear that if the decline in the number of large hotels was not arrested there would be a demand for more industrial development to provide alternative jobs for the staff who worked in them. If that course were followed it could well change the whole character of the town.

An all out effort was at once made to bring as many fairs and exhibitions of national and international repute as possible to the Dome and the Corn Exchange.

Members of a Russian Trade Delegation were invited to the Sussex Industries Exhibition and Trade Fair in 1954 and their much photographed and reported visit secured the town valuable publicity. Another good catch was the first British Manufacturers' Toy Fair. It was a huge success and has been back to Brighton year after year ever since.

Conservatives in conference at the Dome, listening to Prime Minister Winston Churchill.

One of the biggest boosts to the exhibitions business was the opening of Gatwick Airport in 1958. Brighton, an hour from London by rail, was now less than two hours from most of the important commercial centres of Europe by air. Kemp Town's MP, Howard Johnson, told hoteliers that the next link with Europe would be the Channel Tunnel in 1969...

There were exhibitions of a different kind at the Royal Pavilion, the architecturally exotic pleasure palace which in the eighteenth century changed Brighthelmstone from a fishing village to a playground of princes. They were concerned with recreating the splendours of the Regency past rather than getting orders for products of the present.

The Centenary Exhibition of 1950 marked the anniversary of the purchase of the Pavilion by the town from the Crown for £53,000. Many of the state apartments were furnished as they would have been when the Prince Regent was in residence, but it attracted only a few thousand visitors.

It was the Regency Exhibition of Festival of Britain year that brought visitors by the tens of thousands to Brighton. Every day of the three weeks it was open some 4,000 people queued patiently to pay their half crown (12½p) admission fee. In the week before it was due to close the organising committee was inundated with letters, telegrams and telephone calls from people pleading for it to be extended into September.

But they had to be disappointed for the council, not expecting a success of this sort, had promised the Royal Pavilion's banqueting room for a conference booking and had to honour the commitment. However, a modified exhibition was run throughout September, showing the recently restored king's apartments, the north and south drawing rooms, the saloon and the music room.

Perhaps it was a reaction to the restrictions of wartime, which still pervaded the peace, or a need for some colour and culture that brought people from all over the world to the Royal Pavilion in 1951.

Once inside this one-time royal palace they were taken back to an age of glittering extravagance. In the library of the king's apartments the wall decorations had been hand painted to the original design and colour, as had the skyscape motif on the ceiling which was covered with little puffs of white cloud on an azure blue background.

In the king's bedroom was George IV's massive French Empire period writing desk, on loan from Windsor Castle; on the bed a Chinese embroidered quilt given by George IV to Mrs Fitzherbert.

The banqueting hall presented a breathtaking spectacle. The great table, surrounded by twenty four gilt dining chairs upholstered in crimson satin brocade, groaned beneath the weight of gold plate.

The scene of a royal banquet of 1824, from Nash's *Views of the Royal Pavilion,* had been reproduced in exact detail. On the four damask tablecloths, woven for the Regent and depicting scenes of British victories in the Napoleonic and Peninsula wars. were twenty four place settings of silver gilt Coburg pattern knives, forks and spoons. In front of each one there was a fluted and gadroon bordered gilt finger bowl. Here and there on the table, mounted on ivory wheels, were silver gilt double wine coasters embossed with infant figures of Bacchus surrounded by vine leaves through which peered panthers.

For the first time the great kitchen of the Royal Pavilion, where the master chef, Careme, had created superlative dishes for the prince and his guests, could be seen partly restored to its original state. On the scrubbed pine table in the centre of the room was an assortment of poultry, game and fish – all fine examples of the taxidermist's art and supplied by Brighton Museum. Six fat chickens were turning on spits in the huge fireplace.

Once again there were chickens turning on the spit in the great kitchen of the Royal Pavilion, restored to working order.

In the music room was the 33ft diameter circular Aubusson carpet made for Catherine the Great of Russia, and two rosewood grand pianos, one of which had been presented to the Pavilion by Queen Mary.

Among the Hepplewhite and Sheraton satinwood furniture, the portraits, miniatures, the Sevres, Viennese and Russian porcelain, the gold and the silver there was a touch of the macabre – a blood stained trouser leg removed when the first Marquess of Anglesey lost a leg at Waterloo. On show beside it was his artificial leg.

Subsequent Regency Exhibitions ran from the beginning of July to the end of September and some years later there was a move by Clifford Musgrave, the director of the Royal Pavilion Estate, to extend them throughout the year. They were, after all, the town's top attraction.

The Publicity Committee had other ideas. It wanted the music room to be available for conference evening functions until June 30 and throughout September and the banqueting room available for evening functions all the year round. Local organisations complained that they, too, were kept out of the Pavilion by the exhibitions.

In February 1955 the council ruled that the music room, the rotunda, the grand corridor and the banqueting room should the available at all times for conferences and private functions. This allocation argument soon subsided however when the Queen began to return, from Windsor and Buckingham Palace, the hundreds of pieces of the original Chinoiserie furniture which had been removed by Queen Victoria and it became possible to furnish the Royal Pavilion fully throughout the year.

A rather more commercial Regency revival was carried out by Edlins on the sea front between Oriental Place and Montpelier Road in 1954. Where the Abinger family mansion once stood the firm built, at a cost of £125,000, what was

described as 'the first Regency reproduction pub in England'.

Abinger House, pictured above, had oil-fired central heating – another 'first' for this part of the country, it was claimed – and a new type of radiant heat grill in the kitchen.

What Edwardian society hostess Lady Marguerite Abinger would have thought of it is hard to say. She died in her flat in Adelaide Place a year before Abinger House was built. No doubt she would have been pleased that the tradition of hospitality she established at West Cliff House was being continued on the site, albeit commercially rather than socially.

The ban on cross dressing imposed in the last years of the Sussex Arts Ball appears not to have bothered these boys and girls.

8 'A GAY TOWN FROM NOW ON'

LONG before Gay Liberation had been painted on banners and become a cause it had been doing very nicely, thank you, at Brighton, so aptly called the Queen of the Watering Places.

Since the Regency it had been a tolerant place, paying little regard to its visitors' race, religion, creed, calling or their sexual proclivities. If they were interesting and amusing, generous with their patronage and prepared to put on a bit of a show that was all to the good, but they were welcome anyway.

The inscription on the Pylons, put up on the London Road in 1928 to mark the extension of the borough boundary, says it all:

Hail guest, we ask not what thou art.
If friend we greet thee, hand on heart.
If stranger, such no longer be
If foe our love shall conquer thee.

Male homosexuality was illegal until the 1967 Sexual Offences Act permitted it in private between consenting adults aged twenty one and over. The maximum penalty, on conviction, had been a term of imprisonment.

In the Fifties 'the love that not could not speak its name' was still shrouded in Wildean code words or referred to in reports of court proceedings as 'unnatural practices' or 'acts of gross indecency'. Psychologists weighed in with pronouncements about sexual inversion, attributed the condition to unlikely causes and suggested uncomfortable 'cures'.

The attitude of the general public to those it regarded as queers or pansies was, at best, disparaging and at worst, downright nasty. But not in Brighton. The town did not make a fuss about offering a lively but discreet alternative social scene with cafes and clubs, pubs, parks and picking up points for those who preferred concourse with of their own sex.

Exactly when gay replaced queer in general parlance it is hard to say – sometime in the late Fifties, surely? So were the sub-editors responsible for such local newspaper headlines as 'Gay scenes on Royal Pavilion Lawns' on a story about a church garden party totally innocent, or were they playing for laughs?

And what did Brighton Pavilion's MP, William Teeling, intend to convey when he told members of the Brighton and Hove Hotels and Restaurants Association at their annual meeting in 1951: 'There is no reason why we should not make ourselves a very gay town from now on.' This report was headlined: A Gay Town From Now On.

All male comedy shows such as *Soldiers in Skirts* starring Roy Lester, Louis Hayden and Max Carole played the Hippodrome to packed and appreciative audiences several times during the decade.

Then why did members of the council's Watch Committee decide they had better go to the Grand Theatre in January 1954 to see Michael Kim Hartford, who changed from a woman to a man? 'I could not see anything really objectionable in the act' a committee spokesman told the *Sussex Daily News* after seeing the show which, incidentally, the paper did not revue.

Four years later an attempt was made to remove the women members from the Watch Committee. It was not a suggestion of their committee colleagues but of the council's Selection Committee, which gave as its reason: 'The embarrassment caused by the sex films they occasionally have to view'.

The council, which had received protests about this attempt at sex discrimination from two (unnamed) women's organisations, ruled that Alderman Miss Dorothy Stringer, a former mayor and member of the Education Committee for some thirty years, and Councillor Mrs John Hay, should carry on vetting sex films and 'fulfilling all the other duties their male colleagues undertake'.

However the council was not so supportive when an earlier sex bar situation occurred. In September 1950 its transport undertaking had issued an appeal for women conductors to work on the trolley buses as there was a shortage of men.

The local branch of the Municipal and General Workers Union immediately voted unanimously to oppose the appointment of clippies and the six women due to report for work the following Monday were told not to do so.

This incident probably had more to do with money than

with gender. It occurred at the time a bus strike in London seemed likely to spread and when the men's basic way was a mere £4. 17s. a week, which they supplemented by working overtime. They argued that their overtime opportunities would be decreased by the employment of clippies. They could have also argued that it would be equally decreased by the employment of men.

Another gender ban, but a rather more light hearted one, was imposed on the *tres gai* Sussex Arts Ball some years later. Like the Chelsea Three Arts Ball this annual event started in the Thirties and became famous for the parade of floats created by staff and students of Brighton Art College and its midnight cascade of 2,000 balloons.

It was revived after the war and held at the Aquarium Ballroom, usually in October. For months beforehand the date would be advertised in the local papers, coupled with the disclosure that among the 1,500 dancers in fancy dress there would be famous guests 'whose identities will be kept secret until the last moment'.

Fancy the dress certainly was. Boys came as girls, usually long legged, blonde wigged, ostrich feather headdressed showgirls; girls came as boys – top hatted, white tied and tailed. There was sometimes the odd pantomime horse or maybe a many legged Chinese dragon.

Eventually the cross dressing got a bit too outrageous for the staid management of the Aquarium. After all it was a council owned undertaking, the Mayor of Brighton would probably be at the ball, and what would the ratepayers think?

Hence the ban on men dressing as women. It was one easily avoided by the boys who wished to dress as girls. Suddenly there were an awful lot of principal boys and pantomime dames on the dance floor, the latter in final walk down finery rather than comic bust, bustle and an apron.

Real furs were a fashion feature. There were no objections from local animal activists to this 1955 advertisement.

9 ON THE FASHION FRONT

ADOLESCENT males wearing drainpipe trousers, finger tip length jackets, string ties and brothel-creepers – a particularly repellent type of suede shoe with a thick crepe sole – were a Fifties fashion phenomenon.

Never before had young men with a living to earn bothered so much about their appearance. The girls who were with them, jumping and jiving at the Regent and the Aquarium ballrooms, wore black polo necked sweater tucked into the tight waistbands of their full skirts.

The Teddy Boys and their girls represented street fashion. In Brighton there was also beach fashion:

'White cotton panties embroidered with exotic butterflies; salmon pink satin shorts trimmed with cord thigh lacing and worn with a matching jacket and toeless sandals; floral sharkskin briefs flared like a ballet skirt. . .

'On the promenade he (yes, this is from a Fashion for Men feature in the *Brighton Herald* of August 1952) wears jeans or tartan trews with a pretty printed shirt that goes outside, not inside the waistband. To go with the new look haircut – windswept with ducktail flip at the back – must be a white peaked cap or straw sombrero.

'Gay accessories include embroidered waistbelts to set off the hipline and a bandanna kerchief to knot nonchalantly round the neck.'

Bright on the beach the men may have been, but not around the town. The most colourful garment demonstrated by the male models at G H Cobley's fashion show at the Dome in 1959 was a scarlet on electric blue and black dressing gown. There was an all-silk suit in sombre black, a washable raincoat, and a beach shirt and shorts in a pheasant's feather patterned print.

It was the materials of which the clothes were made, rather than their colours and design features, that interested the audience. Men wanted shirts and socks of Terylene or nylon that could be washed, hung up to dry and worn next morning without ironing. And this 'non iron washability' now extended to ties, pyjames, underwear, sports trousers and even light-weight suits.

The *Evening Argus* reported 'a great demand for the latest weatherproof coats in the new Gannex material developed for explorers and now giving windproof quality to the man about town.'

Girls dressed in the daytime much like their mothers – cotton, gingham or seersucker full skirted frocks in summer, coats and skirts, known more commonly as 'a costume', or a skirt and a twin set of matching wool jumper and cardigan in winter.

What they could not get enough of were nylons. Stockings made of this revolutionary material had been introduced to wartime Britain by the American GIs. When they went home the supply almost dried up and women spent hours trying to invisibly mend any ladders in the nylons they had. In London Road an enterprising firm of dry cleaners offered a ladder-repairing service and advertised the fact by having a needle-woman at work in the window.

Even in 1951, six years after the war had ended, the housewives of Brighton were frantically searching their back gardens and the town's open spaces in the hope of finding one of the 200 coloured balloons released from the roof of Peter Robinson's in Western Road on the morning of October 20 to celebrate the shop's opening. Possession of a balloon entitled the discoverer to buy a pair of nylons from the store. Several balloons carried vouchers for free nylons and there were two meteorological weather balloons with free model utility suit and coat vouchers attached.

Contestants in a Holiday Princess competition at the Sports Stadiums show off their charms, and the latest swimwear.

What the housewives did not want was a bright red nylon velvet swoonsuit. This five piece holiday outfit was the brain-child of Brighton's publicity officer, Sidney Butterworth. He commissioned Teddy Tinling, designer of tennis wear for women at Wimbledon, to create a garment which would put Brighton on the fashion map in Coronation year.

The outfit Teddy produced required a controlled striptease by top London fashion model Joy Galloway – 36ins, 24ins, 35ins and height 5ft 5ins – when she demonstrated it at the South of England beauty contest at the Sports Stadium.

Fully clad in all five pieces Joy was dressed for a stroll along the promenade; for cocktails she removed the waist length jacket to reveal a flared skirt and strapless tunic top; with the jacket back on and the skirt removed she was in a playsuit ready for games on the beach; without the jacket the playsuit became a one piece swimsuit; and, wait for it, Joy ripped off the top to cheers from the audience and stood in the spotlight in a bikini of strapless bra and panties.

Red nylon velvet is not the ideal material for beachwear, particularly when each piece is embellished with the letter E in white nylon encrusted with 6,000 rhinestones, tiny mirrors and gold studs in Tudor rose and wheatear design. Patriotic it may have been, practical it was not.

Far more serviceable was the button through dress by Wertheim modelled by a member of William Hill's fashion staff outside the Royal Pavilion in 1955. It had a pin tucked inner vest and skirt and the V neck was finished with a high stand up collar. The model's hat of ostrich feathers had a pompon cockade in shocking pink; she wore the new small Louis heeled shoes; a poppet necklace; and a fur tie made of three skins of barn marten.

Favourite frocks of the Fifties were of Horrocks cotton. Wives of delegates to the Advertising Association's silver jubilee conference had a preview of the manufacturer's summer collection at the Dome in 1958. All the new shapes were on show – the trapeze, the chemise, the harem skirt.

'For eight guineas you can be up to the minute in tomato cotton chiffon with its own underslip,' said the commentator by the catwalk. 'Notice the draw string bustline detail and another draw string threaded just above the knee. . .'

Every January, apart from the epidemic year of 1951, the women of Brighton went sales mad. On January 3, 1950 they started queuing at 5am outside Plummer Roddis in Western Road and there were more than 300 waiting when the doors were opened at 9.15am.

The immediate rush was for fabrics and hosiery, a separate queue forming inside the store for nylons. Utility rayons and cottons were snapped up at four shillings (20p) a yard, as was rayon pique, reduced from 18s 11d (90p) to 2s 6d (12½p) a yard. In the women's clothing department reductions were mainly on non-utility garments. Evening dresses were going for £2 instead of £17; fur coats for £8, down from £37; and top coats for £10.

Six years later the same sales success stories were being repeated. More than 100 queued outside Wades in Western Road on the ninety first birthday of Mrs Olive Wade, then chairman of the company and widow of the store's founder, W J Wade.

Vokins said the spending spree was 'just amazing. . . lots of shoppers from outside Sussex and with household linens, coats and underwear the most popular buys'.

The sales of 1959 broke all previous records and for the first time newspapers reported that in some instances the queues were 'mainly of men.' The Norh Street branch of men's outfitters, G H Cobley, was so packed from the moment its doors opened that the manager had to limit admissions – the people outside having to wait until some of those inside left. At Vokins the greatest crush was again of nylon hunters round the hosiery counter. 'We've served more customers in these sales than in all my fifty years' experience,' said Mr W H Vokins when it was all over.

Harpist Fredrick Alexander, 69, and violinist Joseph Marcantonio, 72, together again after a six week gap in their fifty three year partnership caused by Joseph's illness.

10 GOING SHOPPING

WHEN rationing ended food shops once again became subject to market forces. Butchers no longer had queues of customers waiting patiently for their four ounces of meat a week, with the hope of a rabbit or some offal to eke it out. Grocers ceased to keep delicacies under the counter for special customers, greengrocers began piling up bananas, oranges and other imported fruits on their outside displays.

All kinds of campaigns were launched to bring shoppers into the stores. The London Road and District Traders staged a Shopping Festival in September 1956 and booked Sabrina, the current hot property of British show biz, to open it. Her busty appearance in a silent role with Arthur Askey on television had put her with Diana Dors and Marilyn Monroe among the most popular pin ups.

Hush hush plans were made to bring her to Brighton where she was to tour London Road and be greeted by a musical fanfare outside St Peter's Church. But the organisers forgot that it was Rag Week.

Instead of Sabrina the waiting crowds were treated to the sight of an extremely overblown beauty, with a blonde wig over his short back and sides, waving cheerfully to them from the back of an open car – followed by a mass of motley clad art and technical college students collecting for their chosen charity. Spectators thought that was it and moved away, missing the tasteful display of the real Sabrina's charms which followed some ten minutes later.

Another example of commercial initiative going awry was when the Brighton Wholesale Co-operative Society put up a two foot high stone carving of the borough coat of arms on the front of its new food hall in London Road.

It was told to take it down again as it had not sought

63

Buyers and sellers in Upper Gardner Street in the mid-Fifties

the council's permission to display the arms. 'Permission to use is readily given, but it must be sought,' said a council spokesman.

It was business as usual after the war among the smaller shops around Kensington Gardens but they were no longer all catering, as they did in earlier days, for the less well off locals who came in on foot, by bicycle and bus for bargain priced provisions for their families.

A different sort of customer was coming into the area, one with money to spend, an interest in antiques and a craze for collecting. Of course Brighton traders produced the goods they wanted, as this detailed description of the area in the *Sussex County Magazine* of October 1954 reveals:

'Some confine themselves to single items (blouses, pies, sewing machines) others deal in a maximum profusion of hardware, books and clothing. The proprietors stand in the doorways or confer in the street. . . You can bank in Bond Street, have a perm., buy new neckties or out-of-date collars. In Kensington Gardens you can buy ancient pistols. You can also sell them. This being a lane, excluding by iron posts the intrusion of traffic, is like an arcade without a roof. It is characterised by the aristocratic antique, moulded trash, furniture auctions and fruit.

'Specialities of Gardner Street are biscuits, secondhand records of Monteverdi and classical concertos (no boogie), pastel shaded wallpapers half unrolled, next to the materials required for home made lampshades. On a newspaper stand opposite is a grotesque ballet of puppets (those that are worked by hand) with jolly clown heads and japanesy smocks.

'The spirit of market invades the whole town. In Western Road you may see two gypsy women pushing large prams filled with hundreds of carnations, red white and pink. . .'

There was a lot happening, or about to happen, in and around Western Road. Clearance work started in 1957 in Artillery Street, Cannon Street and Russell Street in preparation for the development of Churchill Square, which was intended to be the shopping and entertainment heart of the town. And in Western Road, in May 1955, the town's first supermarket, Fine Fare – 'believed to be the largest of its kind in Europe,' – opened its doors.

It introduced Brightonians to American style self service with central corridors flanked by double sided display stands containing 15,000 cans of food of all types.

'Every packet, tiny bottle or jar bears its own separate price tag,' the *Brighton Herald* told its readers. 'All perishable food is pre-packaged in hygienic heat-sealed transparent wrapping and kept in the specially designed cool food cabinets which line the walls. Each cabinet has a separate freezing unit which is adjusted to the correct temperature for keeping the contents in perfect condition. A gaily coloured shopping basket is handed to each customer entering the store. . .'

There were cooking utensils, bowls, brushes and other household items for sale on the upper floor of Fine Fare and a 'contemporary style Espresso coffee bar'

Contemporary and coffee bar were virtually synonymous. The design was a sort of practical Scandinavian with added technological twirls. Walls were emulsioned in plain colours or covered with tongued and grooved pine, stained to a deep honey colour. Chairs were of wood or metal, all with straight lines and with seats and back in leather look synthetics.

Frothy coffee, served in Pyrex cups with saucers, was dispensed with a steamy Grrr-swoosh sound from the chrome and glass Espresso machine that dominated the counter. Beside it would be glass shelved display cabinets of packaged biscuits, rolls and cellophane wrapped Kunzle fancies.

By 1956 there were about forty coffee bars in the town, some well run, some not. Most of them catered almost exclusively for the teenage trade, although there was one in North Street that banned anyone under twenty one.

Something nearly all of them had in common, apart from their young customers' conversational exchanges: 'See you later, alligator,' and 'on the Nile, crocodile', was a juke box playing the latest roll n' roll numbers by Bill Haley and the Comets.

The film *Rock Around the Clock*, which had led teenagers to riot when it was shown in other parts of the country, was banned by the Watch Committee in August 1956 although it had not been booked into any of the town's cinemas. If this were intended as a pre-emptive strike it was unsuccessful 'and' commented the *Brighton Herald* 'shows a lack of confidence in the police to deal with any small time hooligans who might

Leesons by the Clock Tower, founded as Sopers Drapery Emporium in 1860, opened as a cafeteria in 1956.

like to show off'.

The film had been screened, without incident, for a week at the Regent the previous month.

At about this time coffee bar owners were denying stories that they operated a ban against French youngsters staying in the town. 'We don't want French newspapers hearing about this as it would hit *Operation Continentale,* the council's new campaign to attract foreign visitors,' said one of them. 'There is no ban on the French although a small number of them have caused a nuisance. We discourage noisy groups in general, whatever their nationality.'

There was music and dancing but no excessive noise or nuisance at the new style luxury cafeteria and restaurant that opened in premises by the Clock Tower, formerly occupied by

Leesons drapers.

The *Brighton Belle*, which had a seating capacity of 350 and eight murals depicting life beside the seaside designed and painted by students of Brighton Art School, was open from 11.45am to midnight. It boasted modern central heating and air conditioning and the fact that all the cooking was done in full view of the customers.

Another move towards fast food was the installation of a large self service slot machine in Western Road. It not only dispensed cigarettes but tins of tongue, slabs of cheese and other snacks, 'all hygienically wrapped in plastic'.

11 CRIMES OF THE TIMES

WHEN it comes to crime Brighton goes for the big ones – trunk murders, race gang riots and, in the 1950s, the Great Conspiracy Case.

It involved the town's Chief Constable, two CID officers, a bar manager and a bookmaker. All five were accused of conspiring together with other persons unknown to solicit rewards for the three police officers and to obstruct and defeat the course of justice.

The townspeople first became aware that all was not well with the Brighton Borough Police Force when newspapers reported the arrival of a team of senior detectives from Scotland Yard to investigate bribery allegations.

I Called in Scotland Yard
says Chief Constable

was the *Brighton Herald's* headline on October 5 1957. This in no way prepared its readers for the shock that was to come when it announced three weeks later:

Chief Constable and
Inspector Arrested

The national newspapers had carried a different disclosure story: 'Report to Cabinet Minister launches police bribery probe' their headlines screamed.

The accompanying articles revealed that Tory MP for Kemp Town, Howard Johnson, had told a Cabinet Minister, unnamed, of allegations of corruption made against the borough police force by prominent citizens of Brighton. The Minister had immediately ordered an investigation by senior detectives from Scotland Yard.

The allegations listed in the nationals were that:

Well known criminals living in Brighton were immune from the law and were tipped off when hunted for their crimes.

Clubs were paying protection money to the police so they could serve drinks out of hours.

Call girl rackets were in operation and the people behind them were paying protection money.

A blind eye was shown to illegal betting houses.

Businessmen were paying for favours from officials in the town.

More than sixty witnesses were called at the committal hearing at Brighton Magistrates' Court. The five accused, Chief Constable Charles Ridge, Detective Inspector John Hammersley, Detective Sergeant Trevor Heath, licensee of Sherry's bar Anthony Lyons and bookmaker Samuel Bellson, all pleaded not guilty.

Among the allegations of the witnesses, fully reported in  the national press with the daily tag: Brighton, a Town on Trial, was that Ridge received £20 a week protection money so the Astor Club in King's Road, where there were so many fights and so much villainy that it was more generally known as The Bucket of Blood, could serve drinks into the early hours without being raided.

BRIGHTON: A TOWN ON TRIAL

Five of these payments, it was said, he received personally and a further fifteen weekly payments of between £15 and £20 were collected on his behalf by Heath from the club's owner, Alan Bennett.

Heath and Hammersley, it was claimed, had obtained money from Bennett after he left Brighton by offering to

Detective Inspector John Hammersley with investigating officer Inspector J Mitchell.

straighten out Bournemouth Police who were interested in Bennett in respect of a crime committed when he was abroad.

They had also come to a gentlemen's agreement with green-grocer Ernest Waite, allowing him to act as a receiver of goods stolen outside Brighton in return for informing on people who brought him goods stolen in the locality.

Heath was also said to have received £68 from Mrs Alice Brabiner, a convicted abortionist, £50 from Mrs Betty Lawrence in whose flat an illegal operation was performed and solicited £10 from James Swaby, a much convicted man, in the cells at Brighton Police Station, not to disclose his previous convictions to the court.

Another allegation against Heath was that he told a police constable on plain clothes duty that he would be paid £10 a week if he kept Samuel Bellson informed when his club, the Lonsdale in West Street, was to be raided.

Bellson, it was claimed, had told wholesale fish merchant Henry Leach that he could straighten out the trouble his son, John Leach, was having over some jewellery he had bought. He told Scotland Yard officers: 'Ridge sent me along to do some business for him but Leach would not pay enough so Ridge went himself'.

When the last witness had left the box magistrates committed the five for trial at the Old Bailey. Attempts were made to have it moved to Lewes Assizes but without success.

There was a twenty day hearing at the Old Bailey at the end of which Ridge quoted crime statistics in his defence which showed that in the four and a half years from 1952 to when he became Chief Constable twenty four drinking clubs were raided.

'In the sixteen months I occupied the position of Chief Constable there were thirty seven raids,' he said. ' And from 1948 to 1956, when I was in charge of Brighton's CID, crimes decreased from 2,183 to 1,674 per annum.

'The number of offences cleared up rose from 43.6per cent to 61.3 per cent and the number of people arrested for criminal offences increased from 453 to 638.'

The jury of ten men and two women found Ridge and Lyons not guilty of conspiracy and Heath, Hammersley, and Bellson guilty. However this was not the end of the affair for Ridge. The comments of the trial judge, Mr Justice Donovan, about his conduct were scathing.

Sentencing the two detectives to five years' imprisonment – Bellson got three years – he told them: 'Neither of you have had the professional and moral leadership you should have had, and were entitled to expect, from the Chief Constable of Brighton, now acquitted.

'If he could contrive, as he did, to go to a suspected briber of the police, in private and alone, it is small wonder that you, Heath, followed that example in the case of Mrs Brabiner.

'If he could admit to his private room a much convicted and hectoring bookmaker and there discuss with him, almost as a colleague, the policy of the police in certain matters, then it is small wonder that you, Hammersley, saw little or nothing wrong in going off on holiday with a local man with a serious criminal record.'

Charles Ridge

The reaction of the borough council's Watch Committee was immediate. The suspended Chief Constable, aged fifty nine and with thirty four years in the police force, was dismissed without pension for being negligent in the discharge of his duties and unfit to hold office.

His fall from grace came a few months after he had planned to glamorise Brighton's police force by introducing a white helmeted, jackbooted police officer riding a grey charger on the sea front in the summer. The horse, named Faithful, had come from the Metropolitan Police and was stabled at Wellington Road.

'Brighton today is vastly improved on what it was ten years ago. . . it is a reasonably law abiding town,' he claimed in his report on crime statistics for 1956.

In this statement Charles Ridge was echoing the opinion of his predecessor, Captain W J Hutchinson, who attributed the decrease in indictable offences in 1955 and increase in the number of arrests 'in no small measure to the readiness with

73

which citizens co-operate with the police'.

There were also a number of other reasons for the generally good behaviour of residents and visitors to the town. Nationally unemployment was running at less than 500,000 and National Service, which did not finish until 1961, occupied school-leavers for two years. There were just not the idle hands about to do evil things – and the borough police force was fully up to strength.

There were some dustups in dance halls between the rival gangs of Teddy Boys. On one occasion a coachload from Southsea, determined to avenge some slight or loss of face incurred at the Regent dance hall the previous week, marched determinedly along Queen's Road threatening retribution on the local lads. They found themselves faced with a solid phalanx of police and wisely decided to go quietly back to the station and home.

There were times when the opposing forces did meet and the dancing would be disrupted as groups of youths, fists, flick knives and feet flying, tried to beat the living daylights out of each other while the band played on. The dance hall managers eventually became tired of their premises being turned into battlegrounds and refused to admit anyone in Edwardian dress.

Another group which came to the attention of the police was the skifflers. When the 6.5 special from London drew into Brighton Station one summer Sunday in 1958 the usual noisy crowd of youngsters disembarked, unslung their guitars and formed up for their customary march to the sea front.

They had been coming down Sunday after Sunday on the same train and disturbing residents by ringing doorbells, chalking slogans on walls and singing wailing hill-billy songs as they paraded through the town.

On this particular Sunday there was a uniformed reception committee waiting for them as they came out of the station.

Like the Southsea Teddy Boys, the skifflers went quietly.

The police action was commended by the *Brighton Herald:* 'The police are employing the effective technique of the Twenties when they used to meet the race gangs at Brighton station and pack them into the next train back to London,' it said in Notes of the Week.

'There are apparently gangs of foolish youths going from town to town and attempting to engage in organised warfare. It is a pity they do not indulge their love of uniform and combat by joining pre-Service units or the Territorial Army. The sergeant major could be relied upon to give them all the exercise they need, although he might not approve of their coiffure.'

The letters columns of the local newspapers were full of suggestions from readers on how to combat the rising tide of juvenile crime. A commando style adventure course 'along the lines of the scheme suggested by the Duke of Edinburgh' was proposed by one group of socially conscious citizens. It would include parachute jumps from balloons to divert delinquents from the path of crime.

Some youth leaders planned to open a coffee bar for the fifteen to twenty one year olds who were not catered for by the 300 or so local youth organisations.

Others called for a super youth club on the lines of the Whisky-a-Gogo in London's Wardour Street, which had a membership of 1,800 and claimed to tame Teddy Boys through offering them high class surroundings and cultural activities 'in tune with young people's interests and outlook'. It had a licensed bar serving everything from Coca-Cola to champagne.

REGENT *Ballroom*
BRIGHTON'S CENTRE OF ENTERTAINMENT

GRAND OLD TYME DANCE
7.30 — 11.   M.C: Mr J A. SHORT
OLD TYME ORCHESTRA
ARCHIE NEWGERITZ and his
Admission 2s. 6d.

AQUARIUM BALLROOM
TEL. 29363

Dates to Remember
MONDAY, SEPT. 19th
Gracie Cole & Her Orch.
MONDAY, SEPT. 26th
The Kirchin Band
FRIDAY, OCTOBER 28th
Sussex Arts Ball
BOOK NOW   BOOK NOW

12 ON STAGE AND SCREEN

BRIGHTON's young, middle aged and old all agreed that dancing was a lovely way to spend an evening. They did so in style in the pre-disco days of big ballrooms and big bands.

Biggest and best ballroom was the Regent, where Syd Dean and his band held sway until 1958 when they moved to the Orchid Room at Purley. The dance floor was under the arched superstructure on the roof of the 3,000 seater super-cinema in Queens Road, built at a cost of £400,000 in the Twenties.

Here there was dancing nightly, all very orderly and well behaved, until the mid-Fifties when the Teddy Boy troubles broke out. Prompt action by the police and the management soon put a stop to these disturbances and it was on with the dance until the end of the decade. In 1967 the ballroom became a bingo hall, six years later the whole Regent complex was closed and a now Boots superstore now sits on the site.

In the years before the war Sherry's ballroom in West Street was a close rival to the Regent but at the end of 1950 it became the Ritz Roller Rink, leaving the Aquarium as the only other ballroom in town offering 'dancing nightly'.

For a short time the Brighton Palais was in operation – one of the top bands of the day, The Squadronnaires, played there in February 1952 – and a few years later the Winter Garden at the Aquarium was inviting people to 'dine and dance in tropical splendour to music in the continental style by Harry, Wally and Fred'.

There was open air dancing on the Palace Pier and the West Pier in the summer and Brighton even had its very own Victor Silvester Dance Studio.

It was opened in 1958 by All-England professional ballroom dancing champions, Dudley and Christine Norton, stepping out to 78rpm recordings of the Victor Silvester Orchestra's playing, in strict tempo, *April Love, All the Way, Stardust, Just in Time* and *Whose Sorry Now.* They encored to Joe Loss's recordings of *Parlez Moi d'Amour, S'Wonderful* and *I Could Write a Book.*

Those who sought serious music, without movement, found it at the Dome. The principal provider of symphony concerts was the Southern Philharmonic Orchestra, under the baton of its own conducter, Herbert Menges, or with distinguished visiting conductors such as Sir Thomas Beecham and Sir Malcolm Sargent.

Brighton Philharmonic Society also sponsored concerts by the London Philharmonic Orchestra with Sir Adrian Boult, Georg Solti and Basil Cameron as conductors and the Hallé Orchestra under Sir John Barbirolli.

Soloists in the 1950 season, for example, included Dennis Matthews, Kathleen Ferrier and Solomon playing the Brahms Piano Concerto No 2 in B flat. That same year there was a lieder recital by Elizabeth Schwarzkopf, a Chopin recital by Niedzeilski, James Roche playing Debussy, and crowd pulling concerts by Yehudi Menuhin and Myra Hess.

Before every household with a teenager had a record player or had even thought about experimenting with stereophonic sound music lovers joined music clubs. There was a large number of them in Brighton, catering for everything from folk to Fauré, choral to contemporary music.

There was also the Brighton Competitive Music Festival, founded in the 1850s and, in the 1950s, having to cope with an average of 4,000 entries involving some 8,500 competitors.

Commercial television started nationally on September 22 1955. In preparation for it Brighton traders begged for a booster station without which the town's 30,000 licence holders would be unable to receive the ITA programmes.

'Many people have bought multi-channel television sets expecting to receive the commercial programmes,' said Mr F W Emery, a representative of the Radio and Television Retailers' Association. 'But they won't be able to because we are blanketed by the Downs.' The would-be viewers stayed blanketed until 1959 when the new transmitter on Whitehawk Hill opened.

BBC television had reached Brighton in time for the Queen's Coronation on May 9, 1953, via the county's first relay transmitter at the old radar station on Truleigh Hill. However some viewers were already receiving cable relay from the Devil's Dyke and viewers on high ground were able to receive other transmissions.

Reception did not become really satisfactory until the Rowbridge station on the Isle of Wight opened in November 1954. Even then there was not a lot to watch. Programmes did not start until 3pm and they finished at 10.30pm with the news – but in sound only.

'We keep within the hours set out by the Postmaster General.. Morning tv will come in time but we can make no definite statement on the matter yet,' said the BBC in a letter to the National Union of Mineworkers ten days before the launch of commercial television.

The television and radio programme listings carried in the *Evening Argus* of September 12, 1955 occupied four column inches (10cm). On the facing page seventy column inches (178cm) were taken up by the display advertisements of Brighton's sixteen cinemas, three theatres, three dance halls, the Ritz Roller Rink and ice skating and ice hockey at the Sports Stadium.

Odd ad out was for a laundrette in St James's Street which offered: 'Your Laundry Washed While You Wait – or go shopping! Soap supplied free. Damp/dry, dried for ironing and fully dry services available'.

A display advertisement for the Ninth Sussex Industries' Exhibition and Trade Fair at the Corn Exchange, admission one shilling (5p), invited audiences to 'Large Screen Television Shows by Richard Burbridge and Co'.

Television as a public, as well as a private form of entertainment, was a feature of the Fifties. Sets were comparatively expensive, cathode ray tubes unpredictable, repairs costly and the technology advancing so quickly that people hesitated about making a commitment.

Many chose to be occasional viewers rather than owners of sets. Evening after evening, regardless of rain and cold, they would stand with their noses pressed to the glass of any tv and radio shop with a switched on set in the window. If a big sporting event were being screened the pavements outside such shops would be packed.

To cater for these enthusiasts what was described as 'the first public tv theatre' was opened by Brighton's own 'Cheeky Chappie', comedian Max Miller, in the autumn of 1953. The 100 seater theatre behind the Esplanade Pavilion, opposite the West Pier, was open daily, including Sunday, and showed continuous tv broadcasts on a screen measuring three feet by four feet.

It took some time for television to make an impact on the size of cinema audiences – continually rising prices, power cuts that interrupted performances, and the growing burden of entertainments tax were having a greater effect. But not in Brighton in the summer of 1950 when dreadful weather was driving holidaymakers away from the sea front attractions and into 'the pictures'.

For a time the queues were back and ticket sales reaching wartime heights but it was a shortlived success. The smallpox epidemic with which the year ended virtually emptied most places of entertainment for months. It was followed by the Rank Organisation's announcement that it intended to cut its

The Odeon at Kemp Town, on the corner of Paston Place and St George's Road, closed in 1960.

cinema managers' salaries because of falling receipts. There were long faces at the town's two Odeons, at the Regent and the 800 seater Academy.

New Home Office regulations for cinemas came into force in 1956. One of the stipulations was that no child aged twelve or under could be admitted after 7pm, even to a U category film, unless accompanied by a person of the age of sixteen or above.

Another, and far more restrictive regulation, was that only cinemas with a rewind room separate from the projection room could show pre-1950 films, which were on flammable stock. Cinemas that did not comply with this requirement had either to make structural alterations or show only new or nearly new films which were fireproof but far more expensive to hire. A number simply chose to close down altogether.

One of the first to go was the 1,200 seater Palladium Cinema on the Russell Street corner of King's Road. It was soon followed by the Arcadia in Lewes Road.

The Paris Continental Cinema in New Road opened, and closed, in an eighteen months period as a direct result of the new legislation. It had been the Dolphin Theatre, changed its name to Her Majesty's Theatre in Coronation year, and in 1955 opened as a cinema showing the sort of unusual and artistic foreign films that were attracting audiences to the Continentale in Kemp Town. Most of them were on pre-war flammable stock and, as the Paris had no separate rewind room, it reverted to being a theatre, staging repertory and revue.

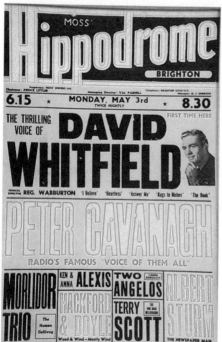

In January 1950 there were four theatres as well as the Sports Stadium staging 'live' shows. The Ballet Rambert was at the Theatre Royal; Ronald Shiner's production of *Worm's Eye View* at the Dolphin; the pantomime, *Cinderella,* at the Grand; another panto, *Sleeping Beauty,* at the Hippodrome and Tom Arnold's ice pantomime *Aladdin* at the Sports Stadium. Plays and musicals were also occasionally presented at the 1,877 seater Essoldo Cinema in North Street.

The cream tiled and stone exterior of the Sports Stadium, which opened as SS Brighton swimming pool in the Thirties.

By the end of the decade only two 'live show' houses were open all the year round. In the summer season the Theatre Royal and the Hippodrome, a Moss Empire house staging twice nightly variety shows, were joined by the Palace Pier Theatre with repertory and summer shows.

The Grand Theatre in North Road had closed in 1955, with the curtain coming down on *The Road Show* starring Afrique. Two years later it was taken over by reproduction furniture maker Bevan Funnell as a factory and warehouse. The building was gutted by fire in June 1961.

Year after year throughout the 1950s summer ice carnivals and Christmas ice pantomimes packed the Sports Stadium and among other attractions were professional tennis, basketball and wrestling.

Former British heavyweight boxing champion Tommy Farr with Tigers coach Bobby Lee.

It was also the home of the famous Brighton Tigers ice hockey team and it was packed to the rafters every time they played there. The team, augmented by star Canadian players and managed and coached by Bobby Lee, won the British League in 1957/8 and the Autumn Cup in 1950/51, 1956/57 and 1958/59. In December 1957 the Tigers beat the Soviet Union's national team 6–3.

One of the Tiger's greatest supporters was former British heavyweight boxing champion, Tommy Farr, who lost to the great Joe Louis in a world title fight in 1937. He had a pub called Tommy Farr's Bar in Queens Road and he also had the Black Lion at Patcham. Tommy tried a comeback in 1950, training for the fight at the Crown and Anchor gym where often champion boxers Don Cockell, Jack Gardner and Terry Allen would drop in for some sparring practice.

The success of the Brighton Schoolboys' Championships and other amateur boxing events encouraged the Sports Stadium management to mount some professional bouts but the response from the public was not encouraging and they were not continued.

Ill health caused Tom Arnold to sell his interest in the ice shows to an American company in 1954. It set up a British subsidiary to run them with Gerald Palmer in charge of production and with former professional world speed skating champion, Benny Lee, as the stadium manager.

Four years later the Sports Stadium was sold to Nicholas Van Slocken and Fred Taylor. They re-launched it as the Brighton Palladium in 1959, reviving the name of the cinema on the corner of King's Road and Russell Street that had closed three years previously.

A series of of Sunday concerts were staged, featuring many of the top stars of the day, among them Shirley Bassey, Ted Heath, Lonnie Donnegan, Cliff Richard, Jayne Mansfield and George Melachrino and his Orchestra.

They were not the sell-out success they were expected to be. Three years later Top Rank took over, changed the name back to the Sports Stadium and closed it down in 1965.

13 FILM STUDIOS AND STARS

WHEN it came to the big occasion or charity event organisers did not have to go out of town for a star of stage, screen, radio or variety to conduct the opening ceremony or be an honoured guest.

Max Miller lived in Brighton, so did Tommy Trinder, Gracie Fields had a house just along the coast at Peacehaven. During Polio Week in 1954 John Gregson, Shelley Winters, Elizabeth Welch, Walter Crisham and Adrienne Corri toured the pubs rattling collecting tins.

After her sensational success in the film *Room at the Top* Hermione Baddeley moved in to a flat in Arundel Road, Kemp Town.

Michael Redgrave was on hand in September 1951 to unveil a plaque to William Friese Green, inventor of the moving picture camera, on a house in Middle Street - No 20b. While he was living there this pioneer of the film industry carried out experiments with colour photography in a studio he had built in the garden.

One of the main reasons for this constellation of stars, to which can be added Googie Withers, Phyllis Calvert, John McCallum, Sam Wanamaker, Jeanne Heal, Peter Butterworth, The Goons and Alfred Marks was the Brighton Film Studios.

They had opened in the red brick parish rooms in St Nicholas Road in 1948 - comedian Sid Field cut the tape - and almost immediately closed for lack of custom.

They might have lasted a bit longer had Councillor Mrs Joan East's plan to use the studios to make a twenty minute short film publicising the town as a holiday resort been accepted by the Ideas Committee.

She read out a scenario she had written for the proposed film, which she estimated would cost £6,000, and members

Film producer Herbert Wilcox and his actress wife Anna Neagle, take a stroll in the gardens of Sussex Square.

agreed to pass the suggestion on to the Publicity Committee. That is as far as it got.

The film studios were revived in 1952 and owed much of their subsequent success to the efforts of their new controller, Herbert Wynne. He had been brought in to reorganise the company and modernise the facilities in the hope that producers would be tempted to leave London and make films in Brighton.

Among the first to do so was the Rank Organisation which leased space at the studios for the production of its

Household Tips features. With the advent of commercial television came bookings for shorts advertising margarine, cigars, washing powder and cold cream.

Film producer Herbert Wilcox, who lived with his famous actress wife, Anna Neagle, at 18 Lewes Crescent, leased space in the studios for three years from 1956. One of Hollywood names he signed, for a series of films for television, was ex-European boxing champion, singer, dancer and cabaret star Carl Brisson. The first of the series, *Romance is Where You Find It,* went into production in March.

It is rather ironic that the film adaptation of Graham Greene's *Brighton Rock,* and a film version of a play about the Prince Regent, *The First Gentleman,* were made before the studios opened. Scenes for the former were shot on Brighton racecourse and for the latter at the Royal Pavilion.

Not long after the studios closed in 1966 film crews spent months in Brighton filming for *Oh! What a Lovely War.* The music hall scenes were shot in the theatre on the West Pier and the battlefields of the Somme were recreated in Sheepcote Valley.

14 RESIDENTS RECOLLECT

IT was fun to live in Brighton in the Fifties. The town had style, it was alive, there was always something to do, somewhere to go, something special about it that set it apart from the rest of the South Coast resorts.

Certainly that is the impression given by the recollections of three former residents who have, in the Nineties, turned back their personal time clocks to recall the town as it was in the middle years of the twentieth century. More vividly than anything else the three remember the food, the fashions and the fun they had.

JUDY MORRIS is the first time traveller, starting with her schooldays at the Convent of the Blessed Sacrament in Eastern Road, next door to Brighton College. She was there in the early Fifties, the last years in which schoolgirls, particularly convent schoolgirls, were expected to behave in public with dignity and decorum.

'We had to wear white gloves and would be sent home if we turned up without them, or with any little detail of our school uniform not totally correct. In summer we were in cream dresses with red collars, panama hats and navy blue blazers. In winter navy blue serge gym slips over white shirts tied at the waist with girdles of red woven material. The nuns did not like it if any girl replaced the girdle with the latest fashion accessory – a red plastic belt.'

The nuns looked even more askance at any association with the opposite sex.

'The windows of classrooms overlooking the college were covered by thick blinds so we would not get a glimpse of the boys. We were strictly forbidden to talk to them should we meet outside. In fact day girls who would normally pass the college entrance on their way to and from home were expected to make a detour round the back streets to avoid doing so. Yet for all these precautions there were quite a lot of pregnancies in the senior school. . .'

Judy moved on to Clark's College to take the GCE examinations that had replaced School Certificate in 1951. 'I was a totally boring teenager,' she insisted. 'All I wanted to do was read books and listen to Beethoven. . . concerts at the Dome, the Carl Rosa Opera Company's visits to the Imperial Theatre in North Street . . . or play seventy eight records on my Regentone radiogram. One Christmas I was given a new record player, with proper speakers.'

'My brother and sister liked big band music, dancing at the Regent and playing records of Lonnie Donegan and skiffle groups.'

It was while she was commuting to London and her job on Amalgamated Press that Judy met the man she was to marry a year later. She waiting at Victoria station in a snowstorm for the 17.10pm to Brighton.

Christopher Moore remembers the occasion in detail:

'It was February 18, 1958. I arrived on platform fifteen and saw a friend of mine, Len Prosser talking to a girl. I went up to say hello to him and the three of us stood talking together, then went to the station cafe for a cup of coffee. After that we stood for a bit longer on the platform before going into the Grosvenor Hotel for a drink.

'A train eventually pulled in at 9pm and we got on it, only to be told at 9.20pm to get off as there was no crew. We finally reached Brighton at ten minutes to midnight.'

The following week the two commuters again found themelves on the same snow troubled trains. A year or so later, on March 19, 1959 to be exact, they were married at St Nicholas' Church in Brighton.

It was a quiet wedding as Christopher's father had died the

Wedding wear in 1959. The bride in white *broderie anglaise* with a short veil, her matron of honour in pink and the bridegroom, with his new three month old nephew in his arms, in a dark suit.

previous week after a long illness. The bride wore a white *broderie anglaise* mid-calf length dress made by her aunt and she was given away by her brother. Her father, an RAF pilot officer/navigator, had been killed when his Lancaster was shot down over Holland returning from one of the thousand bomber raids on Germany.

'Weddings in those days were fairly low key affairs,' said Judy. 'Nothing at all like the lavish dos of today. Except for my cousin, Jill Wix, who had four bridesmaids in red velvet dresses and carrying white muffs, and a huge reception at Hove Town Hall. It was so exceptional that it was the talk of the town for days.

'But we did have fun with the wedding photographs. A few eyebrows were raised when we included the baby in the group but it was really quite in order. My sister Janet, who married the year before I did, was my matron of honour and it was her three month old son, Richard.'

CHRISTOPHER MOORE, demobbed from the RAF in 1950 after service in Kenya, had four days of freedom before resuming his apprenticeship as a letterpress engraver on the *Brighton Herald*.

'After work and at weekends we chaps did what the holiday-makers did – enjoyed all the entertainments Brighton had to offer,' he recalled. 'A favourite spot was the indoor amusements arcade in West Street, which had a couple of juke boxes and we would be-bop with the birds.

'We were then in our early twenties, earning quite good money and with a great interest in motorbikes, and in our personal appearance. I thought my hair was getting thin and remember creeping into Storch's barber's shop to inquire about the treatment advertised in the window to stop hair falling out and to make it grow again.

'The barber looked at me, asked if I had been out east which was pretty obvious as I still had my African tan, and charged me 7s. 6d for a bottle of something that looked like methylated spirit to rub into my scalp. "We will start the treatment next week," he said, but I never went back. Instead I bought a bottle of Silvycrin for one guinea and a Kangol cap to cover my bald spot.

'Sammy Gordon in Trafalgar Street was the tailor we all went to. I paid him £9 for a made-to-measure hound's tooth sports jacket and £4 10s for a pair of trousers. "It's Thursday afternoon and I've been robbed of £2" he cried, as he gave me that amount of discount on the trousers.'

VERNON BRAND was at school at Whitehawk at the start of the Fifties, spending his free time with friends at the Ritz roller skating rink, swimming at Black Rock in the summer, and in the winter watching Brighton Tigers play ice hockey, which he could do for free as he was a Red Cross cadet and in the first aid team.

'I will never forget the excitement at a Tigers v Wembley Lions match in the 1955 season,' he said. 'Tigers were 6-1 down at the start of the third, then it was 6-2, 6-3, 6-4, 6-5. When they made it 6-6 the cheers nearly lifted the roof off the Sports Stadium and the game could not be re-started for a full five minutes. Then we lost 7-6.'

'My first night out with the boys was on Christmas Eve that year. I was taken by my elder brother Richard, who was in the RAF, and two of his friends, to Applejohn's Cider Bar in Market Street. It sold all different types of cider, nothing else.

● ● ● ● ● ● ● ● ● ● ●

FROM THE FAMILY ALBUM:

Vernon at the age of fifteen looking bored on the beach with his parents. 'But I was proud of my new sunglasses,' he said.

● ● ● ● ● ● ● ● ● ● ●

I remember coming home quite light headed.'

When he left school Vernon was apprenticed to A to Z Printers in Queens Road. He had to pass the Army Recruiting Office on his way to work and one day in the summer of 1956 he went inside to sign on.

'Four of us knew we were going to be called up the following year so decided to volunteer earlier. That way we would get more money, and a chance to choose the sort of work we wanted to do.

'We had to take an initiative test, I remember, and Dave went to the Catering Corps, Les to the Royal Artillery and Ted and I finished up in the Royal Engineers.'

While waiting to go into the army Vernon worked for three months as a probationary projectionist at the Essoldo. One of his jobs was to turn on the plenum ventilation system which brought fresh air under pressure into the building to clear the smoke which was often so thick that the screen could not be seen from the projection box.

'One night I did a survey and found I couldn't count up to ten before spotting someone in the audience lighting up a cigarette,' he said.

Vernon and his friends were among the first of Brighton's Teddy Boys.

'My mother was a nurse at Brighton General Hospital and brought me and my two brothers up strictly. No way could I be seen in the house with a DA hair cut, fourteen inch drainpipes of black shiny material with turn-ups, lime green fluorescent socks, blue suede shoes and a Slim Jim tie – we never wore bootlace ties. I had to change into my Edwardian gear at my friend's house in Hanover Street.

'Before returning home I would have to rough up my hair and get back into my ordinary clothes. Usually that meant an open neck shirt, sports jacket, grey trousers and basketball boots.

'Our usual meeting place was the Clock Tower. We would stand on the island waiting for the rest of our lot to turn up. The first time we were in our Edwardian gear half a dozen of us decided to go to the cinema.

'When we were shown to our seats we found our drainpipes were such a tight fit that we could not sit down. Once we bent at the knees it seemed that every seam was about to split, so we had to straighten up and walk out with as much dignity as we could muster. The usherettes thought it really funny but we didn't.'

When home on leave from Hohner Garrison in Germany, opposite the Russian sector of the Belsen concentration camp, Vernon's first port of call was Ma's Record Shop at 1a Guildford Road for the latest David Whitfield releases. Then it was off to Trafalgar Street to Sammy Gordon's or to Bernard Luper to buy the latest in men's fashion for his three week's leave.

'There was nothing to spend money on in Germany and my pay had mounted up. I even bought a car, a black 1939 Vauxhall 10 from Rose Hill Motors near The Level for £160.

'The Regent dance hall was the place everyone went to. Syd Dean played there, it was always packed and I am sure that three out four weddings around that time involved couples who had first met on that dance floor. . .'

A trio of trolley buses in The Steine and, below, a Pullman brake car in original cream and umber livery.

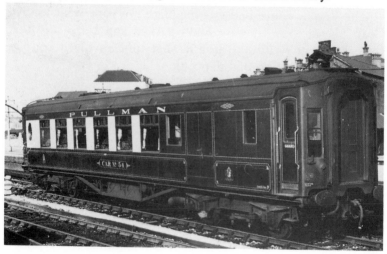

15 TROLLEY BUSES AND TRAINS

THE freeing of petrol from rationing, the increase in the number of car owners and the gradual decline in the number of buses on town and country routes was the Fifties contribution to the national transport problem.

Brighton suffered badly. In 1951 the borough council had the bright idea of banning cars from parking on the sea front between the Aquarium and the Hove boundary. It also wanted taxi ranks and excursion coaches removed from Kings Road.

Cries of protest from hoteliers and other vested commercial interests caused it to think again and two months later it announced that it was buying the Blenheim Hotel with the intention of converting it and the site of the corporation baths in North Street, to a central coach station. Like so many other plans of the period this one also fell through.

Coach traffic reached its post-war peak in June 1952 when 532 coaches arrived in one day. There was not enough room on Madeira Drive for them to set down and pick up, and certainly no space for all day parking.

Over the 1955 August Bank Holiday weekend traffic on the seafront virtually came to a standstill and yet more schemes to cope with the problem were suggested. The then Chief Constable, Charles Ridge, proposed building a raft of concrete over the beach from the bottom of West Street to the eastern end of the fish market hard. Access to it would be by a subway under Kings Road using one of the existing arches near the fish market. The borough surveyor D J Howe, wanted a car park built on the railway station roof.

Neither scheme materialised. Instead on-street car parking restrictions were increased and uniformed traffic wardens with yellow bands on their caps appeared on the streets. They were there, according to the Road Traffic Act of 1956, 'to enforce the law merely by admonishing offenders and pointing out the error they might be about to commit'.

Single and double yellow lines began to appear at the kerb-side in busy areas and so did parking meters. There was just one crumb of comfort for local motorists – in certain streets and near illuminated street lamps, they were allowed to park during the hours of darkness without lights. This concession heralded the end of those cylindrical torch battery powered lights that drivers clamped to the offside window of their vehicles to save draining the battery when parking overnight.

The Fifties were also the beginning of the end of the town's trolley buses. The last one ran on the Patcham and Fiveways route on June 30, 1961 but the service had been halved in March 1959.

Cause of the closure, first recommended by the council's transport committee in 1954, was the rise in costs following the nationalisation of electricity supplies. The trolley buses, which were quiet and quick and popular with the passengers, had a fifteen mile route mileage in 1951 and an excellent safety record. Even when one overturned in Carden Avenue in November that year not one of its twenty three passengers was injured.

The trolley buses, on which the average fare was 1.67d (less than ½p) in 1950, were powered by electricity from the council's own supply and operated at a profit. By 1955/56, with the supply nationalised, the service was operating at a loss.

The motor buses which replaced the trolley buses were in the red and cream livery of the Brighton, Hove and District Omnibus Company or in the green of Southdown, both nationalised concerns. The steady rise in petrol duty, taxes and staff wages was reflected in continually increasing fares and the travelling public had little option but to pay them. But from 1956, when Southdown's annual mileage peaked at 142 million, the decline in passenger numbers was rapid.

It was a chicken and egg situation. When routes that had been profitable became uneconomic the services on them would be reduced. Faced with a long wait between buses prospective passengers looked for alternative ways of getting to where they wished to go. Out came the cars, the scooters, the mopeds and motorcycles. The uneconomic routes became more uneconomic and services were withdrawn. The result was more personal and less public transport.

There was little or no reduction in train services during the decade. In 1951 British Railways advertised cheap day trips to London, leaving every weekday between 9am and 11am and returning on any train, for 8s 6d (43p). Commuters could get a thirteen week season ticket to Victoria or London Bridge for £16 8s.

For those who liked to do the journey in style the Brighton Belle, mothballed or on military service during the war, was

Southdown motor buses, in their two tone green livery, covered and an average of 142 million route miles in 1956

back on platform No 17 at Victoria. Trains with Pullmans ran on the hour from 9am to midnight to Brighton.

The all-Pullman Belle, its umber and cream first class carriages bearing the unexceptional names of *Audrey, Doris, Gwen, Hazel, Mona* and *Vera,* augmented the scheduled service three times a day – at 11am, 3pm and 7pm. Passengers had to pay a supplement of five shillings (25p) on top of the normal fare.

A typical Pullman luncheon menu of the days when the five shilling (25p) limit of restaurant meals was still in force, is this one for March 7, 1950. There is not a vast choice of dishes, but they look impressive in French, and the wines are excellent:

Only one mainline service affecting Brighton was with-

Wines	**LUNCHEON**
Aperitif Ricarlo	Hors d'Ouevre Sainte
Alliance	
Xeres Sec	
Chateau Yquem 1945	Filets de Sole Zena
	Selle d'Agneau du Southdown
Chateau Haut Brion 1945	Petit Pois du Lincolnshire
	Pommes Nouvelles Persillées
	Une Selection de Fromages
	Biscuits Coeurs de Celeri
Martell's Cognac Liqueur	Parfait aux Trois Couleurs
Bols Kummel	
La Invicta Petit Coronas	Cafe Double

drawn under British Railways' rationalisation scheme – the London to Brighton via East Grinstead. It went in 1958, the

100

same year the locomotive works in New England Road closed down completely.

These works had opened in 1852 and built many notable additions to the engine force of the London, Brighton and South Coast Railway and Southern Railway.

First off the production line was a single wheel well tank engine weighing less than twenty five tons. The 1,000th engine, produced in 1947, was the Battle of Britain class 'Fighter Command' which weighed more than 128 tons. Three years later an allocation of orders for the new types of engines required by British Railways was received and the future of the workforce seemed assured. To celebrate, the works were opened for inspection by the public.

But there were shouts of dismay and disapproval when the British Transport Commission announced in 1956 that, because of changes in the method of traction provided by the greater rail modernisation plan, the New England Road workshops would not be needed after the end of 1958 for either construction or repair.

The method of traction referred to was diesel power which was something the Brighton works were not set up to produce. More than 260 men lost their jobs, in spite of union and local insistence that the production line could be adapted to build modern diesels or even railway wagons.

Family transport in the Fifties – the BMW Isetta

16 BUILT IN BRIGHTON

IN May 1957 production started on a totally different sort of vehicle in the main engine shed of the Brighton Locomotive Works. It was the BMW Isetta, described by *Brighton Herald* as 'the first cabin scooter to be manufactured in Great Britain'. The more apt description of bubble car came later.

Negotiations between British Railways and a firm headed by former BOAC pilot, Captain R J Ashley, had started in

January. The part of the nine acre works he wanted to lease was the large shed with the railway line running through it. There he planned to assemble the Italian designed Isetta Motocoupe from imported parts under license from BMW, the German motor manufacturer currently building the little cars in factories in Munich and Milan.

This was not Captain Ashley's first venture in the motor business. In 1946 he had formed the air charter company, Skyways, selling his interest in it four years later to join Armstrong Siddeley at Coventry as a director and general manager. He had given up this secure job with a large company to work on the Isetta project.

Initial production at Brighton was at the rate of ninety cars a week and they were despatched by train to dealers throughout the country, using the line running through the loco shed. It went better than anticipated and soon a workforce of 250 was producing 220 cars a week. Each one took a maximum of sixteen hours to assemble and twenty minutes in the paint shop to receive several coats of colour.

The section of the motoring public that craved economical personal transport could not get enough Isettas, in spite of the relatively high price of £399, which included purchase tax.

The power unit, a 250cc single cylinder BMW motorcycle engine, was robust enough to push the little car along at up to 53mph. As it weighed only 794lbs (360kgs) even with two adults aboard it returned average fuel consumption figures of around 70mpg.

It was extremely easy to park. If there were not room for its 7ft 5ins (2,260mm) length between vehicles at the kerbside its 4ft 6ins width (1,372mm) width could be cheekily fitted in at right angles to the pavement.

Getting in and out was equally easy. The entire front of the car was hinged at the left hand side and opened to a wide angle, taking with it the steering column and instrument panel. It would take two in comfort, if they were good friends, and the foot pedals worked in the same way as on a real car.

Changing gear went with a bang, with or without the use of the clutch. Once first gear was engaged the Isetta would start to roll the instant the key was turned in the ignition. When changing into higher gears the driver could forget the clutch pedal.

The first Isettas were four wheelers but some three wheelers were introduced for countries, including the UK, which allowed them to be driven by the holders of motorcycle licences. Later variants included a 300cc model, a mini van and a 600cc 19.5bhp four seater.

In 1961 Captain Ashley's operation was taken over by BMW and the production line moved to premises in Victoria Road, Portslade. From there three and four wheeled Isettas continued to be produced until 1964.

A more modest motoring venture was launched from a garage in Frederick Place in 1951. It was the Sussex sports car advertised as 'incorporating all the desires of the racing man who in the week wants a comfortable and attractive vehicle for business or pleasure'.

This open two seater, produced at the rate of one every fourteen days, was just one of many hand-made sports specials that were built in the Fifties and powered by hotted up Austin Seven engines.

The Sussex, designed by Peter Brooks, had a top speed of 65mph, an average petrol consumption of 45mpg and carried a price tag of £325. A supercharged racing version with a top speed of 95mph was available at £500.

Brooks Cars also offered to convert 1931–1938 Austin Sevens into Sussex sports specials for their owners for £250. The cars would be finished in pale grey with scarlet wheels and upholstery.

An old established local manufacturing company whose

production line was in top gear in the summer of 1955 was Fryco, makers of fizzy drinks and squashes. The firm began as R Fry and Company in 1874, making aerated waters in a small factory in Middle Street. It bought premises in Park Crescent in 1901 and by the 1930s it had branch factories all round the county and was supplying the whole of Sussex and Kent with lemonades, ginger beers, squashes and other soft drinks.

In the 80°F heatwave in the summer of 1955 Fryco turned out a million bottles of fizzy waters and lemon and orange squashes weekly to slake the thirst of its customers. Although virtually self supporting, with its own printers, carpenters and motor mechanics, it did not make its own bottles or the gas to give the drinks a fizz.

Director and general manager, W H Chatterton, appealed for the Brighton public to return their empties, particularly the large squash bottles. 'There is no shortage of ingredients but there is a shortage of gas,' he said. 'The manufacturers of carbon dioxide are having great difficulty in keeping pace with demand.'

The Darracq that was *Genevieve* with the mayor, Councillor Lewis Cohen, at the wheel at the end of the 1956 run.

17 THE LONDON TO BRIGHTON

LAND'S END to John o' Groats may be longer but London to Brighton has always been the road route most often used by walkers, riders and drivers with something to prove.

It was the best road in the country when the Regency bucks started racing their horses and coaches along it. Then, as now, it followed a fairly direct route from the capital to the coast, covering a distance of fifty seven miles.

Which is probably why it was chosen as the finishing point

for the first Emancipation Run with which pioneer motorists celebrated the raising of the speed limit from four to fourteen miles an hour and getting rid of the man with the red flag.

The run was on November 14, 1896. Thirty three cars set off from Hyde Park at 8am and seventeen of them managed to reach Brighton, the first, a Leon Bolleé steam car, taking two and a half hours to complete the journey. And that, for twenty one year, was that.

In 1927 two national newspapers, the *Daily Sketch* and the *Sunday Graphic,* staged the first run to commemorate the Emancipation Run. In 1930, after the first London to Brighton under the aegis of the Royal Automobile Club, three men met in the Old Ship Hotel on Brighton sea front and decided to form the Veteran Car Club. They were *Autocar's* sports editor Sammy Davies, motorcycle competitions organiser, Jackie Masters, and keen motorist, John Wylie.

From 1934 the RAC has presented replicas of the 1896 Emancipation Run medals to all entrants who reached the Brighton finish in time. In 1951 a total of 147 cars left Hyde Park and 134 finished before the 4pm deadline. A 1904 Cadillac only just made it. The veteran crossed the finishing line in Madeira Drive at 3.58pm, having been pushed for the last one and a half miles by the driver, his two passengers and an AA patrolman in uniform.

A big boost to the the run's popularity, and good publicity for Brighton, where many of the scenes were shot, was the comedy film classic, *Genevieve,* starring John Gregson, Dinah Sheridan, Kenneth More and Kay Kendall. After its London premiere in 1953 police estimated that the number of spectators lining the route of the run at between two and three million. As for the number of cars of all ages – there were almost too many for the A23.

Two years later the London to Brighton had its first American entry – a 1903 Prescott Steamer.

March was, and still is, the month for the Pioneer Motorcycle Run organised by the Sunbeam Motorcycle Club. On the Sunday before the clocks were altered to British Summer Time some 300 machines, the earliest dating from 1897, would make the thirty eight mile journey from Tattenham Corner to Brighton.

In 1951 the winner of the fifteenth run, TT rider Jock West on a 1904 Matchless, arrived half an hour before the first riders were expected and missed a civic welcome. The deputy mayor, Alderman Ernest March, had been told that he should be at the finishing post in Maderia Drive at 11am, not 10.30am, to congratulate the winner.

Cyclists were taking regularly to the Brighton Road, as were the owners of historic commercial vehicles. In 1955 students from the University of Bristol challenged Queen Mary's College, London, to a scooter run from Croydon to the Aquarium to publicise an appeal for funds for an international students centre and hospital.

The following year the Lambretta Scooter Owners' Club organised a series of eight rallies at which there were obstacle races for women only, team events and acceleration and braking tests.

18 A UNIVERSITY TOWN

MOST of the changes that were taking place in Brighton were occurring elsewhere. The town was not alone in having Teddy Boys and tower blocks, coffee bars and bubble cars.

It did, however, decide for itself to have a university. The idea to do so was not new. At the turn of the century a committee and been formed and about £3,000 collected towards founding a university college. The scheme was halted by the First World War and abandoned during the Depression years of the Thirties when the money that had accumulated was used to buy books for the Technical College which offered degree courses in the arts and sciences.

In 1956 the Director of Education, William Stone, revived this earlier idea of making Brighton a university town. He organised a series of lectures by distinguished academics on the desirability of doing so and prepared a memorandum on the matter for the Education Committee.

In June that year the council considered his proposals and used them as the basis of a scheme it passed on for government approval. In anticipation of success it granted the proposed university a 999 year lease on Stanmer Park at a nominal rent of £1 a year. It also agreed to make £12,000 a year available to it in its early stages of development and to grant it rate relief.

Someone else who anticipated Brighton's emergence as a university town was Helena Normanton QC, the first woman barrister at the English bar and one of the first two women in the country to take silk. In February, months before the scheme came before the council, she sent a cheque for £5 to the Director of Education, as a 'first contribution to the new university'.

After her death in 1957 her will revealed she had left £20,000 towards the establishment of a university in Brighton.

The University College of Sussex came into being in 1959 and started work with fifty undergraduates in three houses at Preston. At the same time a start was made on new buildings in Stanmer Park, designed by Sir Basil Spence. Falmer House, the principal building of the complex, was completed in 1963, a few months before the University College became, by Royal Charter, the University of Sussex.

Illustrations

Illustrations

Select bibliography

Brighton Gazette Year Books 1950–1953

Britain 1945–1970 by L A Monk, G Bell and Son, 1976

Daring Hearts, Lesbian and Gay Lives of 50s and 60s Brighton by Peter Dennis, Beccie Mannall, Linda Pointing, QueenSpark Books, 1992

Encyclopaedia of Brighton by Timothy Carder, East Sussex County Libraries 1990

Life in Brighton by Clifford Musgrave, Faber and Faber 1970

Sussex County Magazines, 1950–1956

Sussex Police Authority press cuttings, photographs albums and register of clubs 1946–64. At East Sussex Records Office

The Old Ship, A Prospect of Brighton by Raymond Flower, Croom Helm 1986